essential guide to
cake decorating

This is a Parragon Book

First published in 2005

Parragon
Queen Street House
4 Queen Street
Bath BA1 1HE, UK

Copyright © Parragon 2005

Designed, produced and packaged by
Stonecastle Graphics Limited

Text by Alex Barker
Cake designs by Alex Barker
Photography by Steve Moss
Edited by Bridget Jones
Designed by Sue Pressley and Paul Turner

With special thanks to Lynne A. Strafford for her cakes and
cake inspirations and to Kenwood for the loan of the latest
Kenwood Major.

ISBN 1-40545-015-0

Printed in China

Using this book

• Use either metric or imperial measures, not a mixture of both
in any one recipe.
• The following abbreviations for spoon measures are used
throughout: tsp = teaspoon; tbsp = tablespoon. These refer to
measuring spoons, not cutlery. All spoon measures are level
unless otherwise stated.

$1/4$tsp = 1.25ml
$1/2$tsp = 2.5ml
1tsp = 5ml
1tbsp = 15ml

• For best results when making light cakes, use free-range eggs.
• Oven temperatures are for standard appliances. Please check
the manufacturer's instructions for your oven, particularly for
different types of fan or fan-assisted ovens.
• Use cooking times as a guide: results may vary slightly in
different ovens and this may make a difference when baking
cakes. It is a good idea to make a note of any slight variations
in cooking times in your oven for optimum results.
• Recipes using raw or lightly cooked eggs should be avoided by
infants, the elderly, pregnant women, convalescents, and anyone
suffering from an illness. If you make cakes for gifts or for public
occasions or are worried about the use of raw egg in marzipan
or royal icing, buy dried egg products instead. These ingredients
have been heat treated to ensure they are safe. Alternatively, buy
marzipan or icing.
• Follow the instructions carefully.
• Safety is very important – children should always be supervised
by a responsible adult while in the kitchen. Sharp tools, such as
knives and scissors, and small objects, such as icing nozzles
which could cause choking if swallowed, should be kept out of
the reach of young children.
• The publishers and their agents cannot accept liability for loss,
damage or injury however caused.

essential guide to
cake decorating

Alex Barker

p

Contents

Introduction

Queen Victoria's desire for a piece of cake in the afternoon led not only to the creation of the Victoria sponge but also to the very English 'teatime' interlude. In the 21st Century, teatime often still means 'cake' and even though we rarely make time for tea in the old-fashioned way, most of us will not turn down the occasional offer of a slice of cake. However, turning an everyday cake into a glamorous gâteau or a crazily decorated party piece requires a little more than just baking.

Cake decorating can be a craft, a hobby or even a business. The skills used at the highest level of sugarcraft require training, practise and expertise. Most of us simply want to enjoy being creative, and taking pride in making something really special or unusual. Making a beautifully decorated cake for someone, or for a family occasion, is a real gift of love and time.

Today's cakes are as simple and stylish, or as colourful and daring as you want them to be. Finding the right design or idea is the first most important stage – frills, ribbons and roses suit some occasions; a brightly coloured design with edible caricatures another; or fresh or frosted flowers or fruits may be appropriate. You may well be surprised how easy it is to make a creative cake if you take the time to select and plan a design. Look around at the tools available to turn an idea into reality.

The *Essential Guide to Cake Decorating* describes all you need to know about simple stylish cake decorating, from the basic cake recipes to a range of stunning designs. The first half of the book covers the recipes, techniques and skills that will equip you to make any of the cakes with confidence. Whether you want a Victoria sponge, a dark fruit cake or other favourites, like rich chocolate cake or carrot cake, they are all here. Professional tips, guides to quantities for making larger cakes and information on choosing the right equipment are all included. Learn how to use classic methods for marzipan and royal icing, or soft sugar paste for exciting effects.

The second half of the book leads you carefully, step-by-step, through the stages in making 24 beautiful cakes. It doesn't matter how inexperienced you are, the techniques and guidance in the early pages will show you all you need to know. Discover elegant designs based on surprisingly simple piping; model charming little penguins; or succulent-looking raspberries and blackberries. Alternatively, try your hand at pretty delicate butterfly run-outs or stunning bronze cut-out doves. Why not simply have fun with the family, making fabulous fairy cakes for tea?

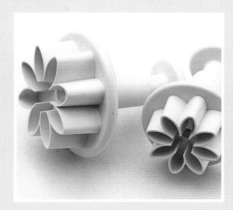

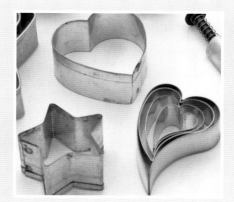

Planning Perfect Cakes

There is such an array of recipes, designs, equipment, tins, gadgets, ingredients and colours that making the right choice is the first important step. If possible, start with a design outline, then collect everything needed to make and complete the cake. If you have a specialist cake decorating supplier on your doorstep you are lucky; if not, allow plenty of time for mail order delivery of any special cutters, colours or cake boards required.

As well as a reliable recipe, turning out a great basic cake demands a good tin, prepared properly, and an oven that cooks evenly and steadily at the right temperature. Generally, there's no need to buy a new tin if you already have one of the correct size and shape – simply take care to line it properly. Tins of unusual shape or size are available to hire from catering shops or specialist cake suppliers. Make a point of keeping all your cake-decorating tools stored safely together, for example in a toolbox. Many items are tiny, easily lost and costly to replace.

Baking Equipment

Most cooks already have a selection of baking equipment, often handed down through generations, and few have to buy everything from new. However, using the right item for the job does make all the difference, especially when it comes to baking tins and mixers.

- **Boards:** If possible use separate boards for general cooking and making sugar decorations. Small white (or coloured) smooth plastic boards are available from specialist cake decorating shops.
- **Brushes:** Use a variety of sizes for greasing tins, brushing on apricot glaze, moistening surfaces with water or lemon juice, and painting fine designs.
- **Cake boards:** Available in many sizes and shapes, thin or thick, in both gold and silver,
- **Cake tins:** Available in all sizes and shapes. Choose good-quality non-stick tins with loose bases. Keep your tins really clean and dry. Hire unusual shapes or large sizes for special occasions.
- **Cooling racks:** Cool cakes and bakes on wire racks.
- **Knives:** Palette knives, both large and small, are important for spreading, smoothing and flattening. You will also need a selection of good, sharp cook's knives for cutting and trimming cakes.
- **Mixers:** If you frequently make cakes you will find a good mixer indispensable. An electric hand-held mixer is the most economical and useful for creaming light mixtures, whisking eggs or whipping cream. A large free-standing food mixer with beater and whisk is ideal for frostings, royal icing and fruit cakes. Food processors are not ideal for cakes or icings unless they have a whisk blade and a slow speed setting for gentle mixing.
- **Papers and wraps:** You will need greaseproof paper and non-stick baking parchment to line tins, draw designs or make piping bags. Cling film keeps icing and marzipan soft and airtight. Foil is a good base on which to set chocolate and caramel designs. Kitchen towel can be used to support shapes and dry items.
- **Sieves:** For sifting flour and sugar; also for finely dredging cakes with icing sugar or cocoa powder.
- **String:** To tie paper around cake tins when baking rich fruit cakes, to protect them from over cooking on the outside; also useful for measuring tins or cakes of awkward shapes.

Pictures left, from top:

A good mixer will save a lot of hard work.

- *Use brushes to keep surfaces clean, grease tins or paint decorations. Tweezers and scalpels allow pin-point precision on fine cakes.*
- *Keep cutting knives sharp. Have a good selection of palette knives to move even the smallest item with care.*
- *Good-quality tins cook evenly and clean easily; cakes will also come out easily.*
- *Cake boards can be used in many ways and can be covered with sugar paste or pretty paper to suit your design.*

Lining Cake Tins

Preparing a Round Tin for a Fruit Cake

1 Cut two circles of greaseproof paper for the base and a strip twice the depth and just larger than the circumference of the tin. Fold in half lengthways and make a 2.5cm (1in) fold along one edge of this strip. Make angled cuts into the folded edge.

2 Place one circle in the base of the tin, then line the inside with the strip, cut edge down. Overlap the cut edge to to curve it neatly.

3 Place the second circle of paper in the tin to cover the overlapping cuts around the edge. Lightly grease the base and sides.

4 Tie a band of double-thick brown paper around the outside of the tin. Place the tin on folded newspaper or brown paper on a baking tray.

Lining a Swiss Roll Tin

1 Cut a rectangle of greaseproof paper 5cm (2in) bigger than the tin on all sides. Place the tin on the paper and cut into the corners so the paper overlaps neatly in the corners.

2 Grease the tin lightly so the paper sticks. Place the paper in the tin, grease lightly and sprinkle with flour. Shake off the excess flour before filling with sponge mixture.

Icing and Decorating Equipment

The tools needed for icing and decorating can be extensive, especially if you are clever and creative, and enjoy producing elaborate and artistic cakes. There are always new tools and shapes of cutters on the market, available through specialist websites, so you don't even have to go out to update your toolbox!

• **Colourings:** Edible food colours are available in several forms. Liquids are best for pastel shades; pastes for stronger, deeper shades; dusting powders can be brushed on to give subtle effects; and coloured pens can be used for small areas of writing or drawing instead of using a paintbrush.

• **Crimpers:** These resemble wide tweezers with shaped ends that imprint different shapes (such as hearts, leaves or scrolls) instantly onto the top or bottom edge of a cake or in rolled-out sugar paste.

• **Cutters:** There are dozens of shapes available: novelty animals, festive shapes, numbers and letters, specific types of flowers and petals – so you can stamp out almost any design.

• **Edible glue:** Ideal for assembling flowers or attaching designs to sugar paste.

• **Embossers:** These look like small pencils and are used to press simple patterns onto icing or sugar paste. Similar effects can be achieved with small graters, or zesters, and patterns can be pressed on using pieces of textured materials and mesh.

• **Floristry wire:** This is perfect for attaching leaves to flowers or making a bouquet, and ideal for giving ribbons some shape or fixing festive party decorations.

• **Flower Finishes:** You can buy tiny stamens and various types of coated wires for stamens. Veining tools give a realistic effect to cut-out sugar paste leaves.

• **Flower Nail:** A base on which to pipe tiny simple royal icing flowers.

• **Modelling tools:** A dog bone tool and ball tool help give the perfect shape to sugar paste designs. Available in various shapes and sizes.

• **Piping bags:** Small nylon washable bags are available in several sizes, but if you are using several different colours of icing for fine piping, or small quantities, then paper bags are much easier to use. Buy a batch in bulk or make your own (page 35).

• **Piping nozzles:** There are hundreds of small nozzle shapes for fine royal icing piping, from fine writing to butter icing shells. Buy a small selection of the basic types first, and then gradually add shapes as you become more adventurous.

Pictures left, from top:

• *Edible colours are available in paste, powder, liquid or as pens. Edible gold or silver, glue and varnish are also useful.*

• *Buy tools as you need them – there will be one for every shape and technique.*

• *Tiny shapes that you can then paint or dust over are easily imprinted with embosser pens, which are available in many different designs.*

• *Piping nozzles can produce delicate lines, and a sugar paste gun makes rope designs in seconds. String is used to tie brown paper around a prepared fruit cake tin and is useful for measuring cake sizes when rolling out marzipan or sugar paste.*

- **Ribbons:** Add a simple touch of colour with a ribbon sweeping around the cake or dressing the edge of the board. Ribbons can be dramatic, in both colour and style, for that final touch.
- **Rolling pins:** Marzipan and sugar paste require a standard-size rolling pin, completely smooth for the best result, but for small shapes and flowers a very small marble, plastic or steel rolling pin is useful. There are also patterned rolling pins to emboss paste as it is rolled out.
- **Ruler and scrapers:** Straight-edged metal rulers are used to flat ice the top of a cake and give a perfect, smooth surface. Some rulers have comb-ridged edges to apply a quick finish to the top or sides. Scrapers are short and wide, usually about 10cm (4in) long, for smoothing excess icing off the sides of a cake or board.
- **Scalpel:** For cutting paper designs or fine edges, or carefully inserting or removing items in a design.
- **Scissors:** You may need both tiny and large scissors for different tasks.
- **Shapers and smoothers:** For a professional finish you can buy a smoothing tool but for tight corners and short cake sides the simplest, effective way to smooth sugar paste is to use a chunk of spare paste wrapped in small polythene bag or cling film.
- **Sponges:** Raised items in run-out icing or sugar paste often need supporting until set and a tiny corner of sponge is perfect for this task. Remember to remove the sponge when the item is dry.

- **Sticks:** Cocktail sticks or small wooden sticks can be useful for shaping, supporting, or frilling edges.
- **Sugar paste and icings:** Sugar paste, flower paste, modelling paste, pastillage, royal icing, run-out icing and many more types are available mixed or in a ready-to-mix powder form from sugarcraft specialists. To make some pastes and icings you may need specialist ingredients such as glycerine, glucose, gum tragacanth or gelatine.
- **Sugar paste gun:** A gun or pump with discs to extrude various shapes of sugar paste or marzipan.
- **Turntable:** The ideal equipment to raise and turn a cake for easy decorating. Some can be tilted.
- **Tweezers:** Invaluable if you have to remove the tiniest crumb from the top of a cake, or to place a very delicate decoration precisely.

The Finishing Touches

The right finishing touches are necessary to create a fabulous cake. Choosing the right board – shape or colour – is just part of setting the final scene. Trimming with ribbons, scattering flower petals, adding table décor such a stars, or dragees, wrapping or sitting a cake in tissue are all examples of ways to add to the total effect. The choice of trimmings in the shops is endless, so have fun staging your cake as well as making it!

Pictures right, from top:

- *Cutters come in many different shapes, some in sets of various sizes. For more adventurous designs try the larger flower sets for shapes such as sunflowers or lilies. Once cut, you can shape the paste to give a very realistic result.*
- *Ready mixed paste or powders give exactly the right icing consistency. Most are white, but some are available in different colours.*
- *Decorations for finishing a fabulous cake include colours, candles, crackers, dragees, papers, party poppers, ribbons, sparklers, streamers – the list is endless.*
- *A turntable is a very good investment for cake decorating.*

Recipes for Success

Using the very best ingredients is the base of any good cake. For example, sponge cake especially, benefits from the use of fresh free-range eggs for their rich golden colour and light-as-air texture. Fruit cakes benefit from good dried fruit that is full of moist richness. Use good quality vanilla essence – not synthetic flavouring – particularly for delicate sponges in which its distinct warm flavour sings through.

Use equipment wisely: a food mixer can save time and effort but be aware of the potential for over mixing. A light sponge needs a light touch for a well-risen springy result. The initial creaming of fat and sugar to a pale fluffy texture helps the ingredients for a fruit cake to mix well. Beating royal icing to a thick glossy cloud can be very tough on your wrists.

Discover the right techniques that result in the perfect finish. Whether you prefer working with classic royal icing or the more immediate, hands-on sugar paste, the following pages have lots of advice and tips to share.

Sponge tips

- To test if a sponge cake is cooked, press gently on the top with your finger tips. If the imprint quickly disappears, the sponge is cooked.
- Listen to your sponge and if it is still crackling furiously it is not fully cooked!
- For a really light Genoese sponge, sift the flour three times to incorporate plenty of air and whisk the eggs over a pan of hot water.
- To freeze a sponge, cool thoroughly. Double wrap in cling film and then in foil. Allow 1 hour to thaw, but if cutting into layers do this while still part frozen.
- Using a food processor to make a sponge takes a matter of minutes and the only difference is that it will not be quite as light and fluffy as the hand-mixed version. Simply mix everything together in the machine on its slowest speed for as short a time as necessary. When well mixed, spoon into the tins.

Variations
quantities for a 3-egg mixture

- **Lemon or/orange:** Add 2tsp orange flower water, or the finely grated zest of 1/2 lemon or orange with the egg yolks.
- **Chocolate:** Replace 1tbsp flour with sifted cocoa powder and add 1-2tsp extra sugar.
- **Nuts:** Replace 25g (1oz) flour with an equal weight of finely ground almonds or hazelnuts.
- **Coffee:** Dissolve 2tsp instant coffee in 1tsp boiling water and blend in with the eggs.

Simple Sponges

Making a good plain sponge cake does not require impossible skill, simply the right recipe and a little time. A sponge can then form the base for a wide variety of other cakes, from fairy cakes to fruit gâteau, novelty shapes and elaborately decorated celebration cakes. Cake trimmings can be used in wonderful weekend puds. A sponge is the most versatile cake to have in your repertoire.

Victoria Sponge

The basic proportions of a Victoria sponge are well worth remembering so you can whip up this popular family cake at a moment's notice. One hour from start to finish is really all it takes – even less if you use a food processor.

Serves 4-6

175g (6oz) butter or margarine, softened
175g (6oz) caster sugar
3 eggs, lightly beaten with 1-2tsp
    vanilla essence
175g (6oz) self-raising flour, sifted

1 Preheat the oven to 180°C/350°F/gas mark 4. Lightly grease the base and sides of one 18cm (7in) cake tin, or two sandwich tins. Line the base with paper and grease this.

2 Cream the soft butter and sugar in a mixing bowl until pale and fluffy. Gently beat in the eggs and vanilla, gradually adding the flour.

3 When the ingredients are smoothly combined, without too much beating, place the mixture in the tin or divide it evenly between the two tins. Flatten the top or tops with a wetted knife and place in the middle of the oven, on the same shelf if possible, when baking two cakes.

4 Bake for about 20 minutes. The cooked cakes should be light golden, well risen but flat on the top and springy to the touch. Leave to part cool in the tin on a damp cloth for speed and then turn out onto a cooling rack and leave until cold.

Victoria Sponge Proportions for Tin Sizes (one deep tin or two sandwich tins)

15cm (6in) round tin: 110g (4oz) each of fat, caster sugar and self-raising flour to 2 eggs
18cm (7in) round tin: 175g (6oz) each of fat, caster sugar and self-raising flour to 3 eggs
21cm (8in) round tin: 225g (8oz) each of fat, caster sugar and self-raising flour to 4 eggs

Note

Remember that cooking times may vary depending on the oven used. Cake mixture in one deep tin will take longer to cook than when divided into two tins. Use cooking times as a guide.

Genoese Sponge

The Genoese sponge (*Genoise* in French) is a whisked sponge with a very light open texture. Whisked sponges can be fatless, but a little melted butter is added to a Genoese for a richer result and improved keeping qualities. This type of sponge is used for Swiss rolls, sponge fingers, sponge flans and layered gâteau. It is very quick to cook and impressive to serve.

1 Preheat the oven to 180°C/350°F/gas mark 4. Grease and line one 23cm x 35cm (9in x 14in) Swiss roll tin, or two 18cm (7in) round sponge tins.

2 Sift the flour and salt together two or three times for a really light result.

3 Place the eggs and sugar in a large mixing bowl and whisk, with an electric beater, for about 10 minutes or until the mixture is really thick, creamy and pale. A trail should be left in the mixture when you lift out the beaters.

4 Use a large spatula to fold in the sifted flour and melted butter, carefully and gently folding until smoothly mixed. It is vital to fold in all the flour evenly but try not to overmix as this will reduce the lightness of the sponge.

5 Pour into the prepared sponge tins and bake for 10-12 minutes, until pale golden, just firm to the touch but very springy. Leave in the tin to cool for 3-5 minutes then transfer to a wire rack.

Makes one Swiss roll or two 18cm (7in) sponge cakes

100g (3¹/₂oz) plain flour, sieved
pinch of salt
3 eggs
100g (3¹/₂oz) caster sugar
1tbsp melted butter

Rolling Swiss Roll

1 While the sponge is cooking, place a clean tea towel on a flat surface. Cover with greaseproof paper and add a good sprinkling of caster sugar. Invert the freshly-baked sponge carefully onto this. Gently remove the baking paper.

2 Trim any crisp or uneven edges. Make a shallow cut 2.5cm (1in) in from the narrow edge of the sponge for easy rolling.

3 Cover with a clean sheet of greaseproof paper. Use the tea towel to help roll up the sponge, folding the paper inside. Leave until really cool.

4 To use, gently unroll and spread with filling (don't add too much). Gently re-roll the sponge, using paper or a tea towel as support. Place join-side underneath – on a board or serving plate and decorate as required.

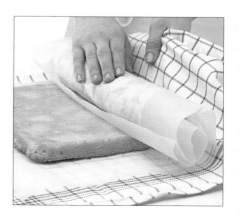

A Simple Decoration for Sponge Cake

Sifting icing sugar over a template makes a very quick, simple and stunning decoration. The easiest option is to sift icing sugar over a paper doily, preferably one with a wide and open design. Alternatively, you can make a template by drawing a pattern on clean card or greaseproof paper and cutting it out neatly. Be generous with the sugar to give a strong design or colour the sugar with edible powder colours.

There's no need to reserve this star design for Christmas as it is ideal at any time. Find the template on page 96 and use only the centre part for smaller cakes.

1 Dredge the top of the cake with icing sugar. Place the central star and outer circle templates in position, laying them gently over the icing sugar. Dredge with cocoa.

2 Use tweezers and a palette knife to remove the central star, taking care not to spill cocoa on the icing sugar.

3 Remove the outer circle template and transfer the cake to a plate.

Madeira Cake

The Madeira cake evolved from the American pound cake, originally made with a pound in weight of each ingredient. It has become popular (known by various names) all around the world. It is a longer-keeping, firmer cake than a whisked or Victoria sponge. It is ideal for those who do not like rich fruit wedding cake, is perfect for making gâteau with several layers, and it freezes very well. Often baked in a loaf tin, it is a delicious, simple teatime cake, especially if you add a warm sugar and lemon crusted topping.

Madeira Tip
• To test if a Madeira or any deep Victoria sponge or light or rich fruit cake is cooked, push a metal skewer into the middle. If it comes out free of sticky mixture, the cake is ready.

Variations
quantities for a 18cm (7in) round or 15cm (6in) square cake
• **Lemon or orange:** Add the grated zest of 1 orange or lemon, or 1tbsp orange flower water.
• **Nuts:** Replace a quarter of the flour with finely ground nuts of your choice.
• **Seeds:** Add 2tbsp poppy, caraway or mixed seeds.
• **Cornmeal or Polenta:** Replace up to half the flour with ready-to-use cornmeal or polenta.

Makes one 18cm (7in) round, 15cm (6in) square or 1kg (2lb) loaf cake

200g (7oz) butter or margarine, softened
200g (7oz) caster sugar
3 large eggs
225g (8oz) plain flour, sifted
1$\frac{1}{2}$ tsp baking powder
salt
1$\frac{1}{2}$ tsp vanilla essence (optional)

1 Grease and line an 18cm (7in) round cake tin, or 15cm (6in) square tin or 1kg (2lb) loaf tin. Preheat the oven to 180°C/350°F/gas mark 4. Beat the butter or margarine and sugar together until light and creamy. Gradually beat in the eggs until evenly blended.

2 Mix the sifted flour, baking powder and salt and fold in gently using a large metal spoon. Add vanilla if required. Spoon the mixture into the prepared tin, level the top and bake for 1¼ hours, until a skewer pushed into the middle of the cake comes out clean and free of sticky mixture.

3 Remove the cake from the oven and leave to partly cool in the tin for 15–20 minutes. Then turn out onto a wire rack and leave to cool completely.

Slicing a Madeira or Sponge Cake

To slice a Madeira or sponge cake into several layers, allow it to cool completely. Chill a sponge briefly or Madeira for several hours if you need a fine, crumb-free cut. Place on a flat base – on a turntable if you have one – and place a sheet of greaseproof paper on top so you do not leave finger indents. Use a large, sharp knife. Cut partly through, then give the cake a quarter-turn, keeping the knife in place, and continue cutting. Turn again and continue cutting until the cake is sliced through. The knife remains in the same position to produce even layers.

Madeira Tip

• Madeira cake freezes well so make double quantities. Bake one quantity in a rectangular or square tin, and freeze it in slabs or sections. Use it for Iced Fancies (page 56) or for quick family puddings.
• Plain cake trimmings are great crumbled into a fruit crumble dessert topping.

Lemon Sugar Topping

Use this variation to make a simple weekend cake that may well be eaten before it has time to cool! Spooning the topping over takes seconds and it does not need a rich filling. Bake the cake in a loaf tin so it is easy to slice.

While the cake is still warm and in the tin, pierce it with a skewer, several times right the way through. Warm the lemon juice and syrup together. Add the sugar and immediately spoon the mixture over the cake, so the flavoured syrup soaks through leaving some of the sugar crystals on the top.

4tbsp lemon juice
1tbsp golden syrup
2tbsp granulated or preserving sugar

Madeira Proportions for Tin Sizes

Tin	Fat	Caster Sugar	Eggs	Baking Powder	Plain Flour
18cm (7in) round or 15cm (6in) square	200g (7oz)	200g (7oz)	3	1½ tsp	225g (8oz)
20cm (8in) round or 18cm (7in) square	250g (9oz)	250g (9oz)	4	2tsp	350g (12oz)
23cm (9in) round or 20cm (8in) square	350g (12oz)	350g (12oz)	6	2½tsp	450g (1lb)
25cm (10in) round or 23cm (9in) square	400g (14oz)	400g (14oz)	7	3tsp	500g (1lb 3oz)
30cm (12in) round or 28cm (11in) square	500g (1lb 3oz)	500g (1lb 3oz)	10	4tsp	675g (1½lb)

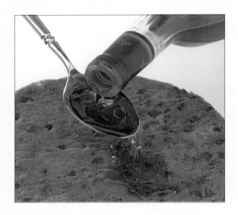

Fruit Cakes

A good home-made fruit cake is a rare treat these days, and festive occasions are incomplete without one. Why not make a small or individual fruit cake for a thank you or birthday gift for a special friend? It is better than any gift you might buy!

Dark Rich Fruit Cake

This dark and rich cake is made with dark ingredients – brown sugar, treacle, dark fruits – and traditionalists used to add gravy browning to ensure it was really dark! It is usually 'fed' with brandy before icing and can be kept for months, even years, thoroughly wrapped and stored in a cool dry place.

Makes one 20cm (8in) square cake or 23cm (9in) round cake

900g (2lb) mixed dried fruit
110g (4oz) chopped mixed peel
110g (4oz) glacé cherries, chopped
110g (4oz) pitted prunes, chopped
2-3tbsp sherry, brandy or rum
grated zest of 1 orange
grated zest of 1 lemon
350g (12oz) plain flour, sifted
1tsp ground cinnamon
1tsp ground mixed spice
1tsp salt
5 eggs
275g (10oz) butter or margarine, softened
275g (10oz) soft dark brown sugar
1tbsp treacle or golden syrup
Extra brandy to moisten the cooked cake

1 Prepare a 20cm (8in) square or 23cm (9in) round tin (page 11). Preheat the oven to 160°C/325°F/gas mark 3. In a large bowl, mix the dried fruit, peel, cherries and prunes with the sherry and orange and lemon zest. Leave to soak for 1–2 hours if possible to let the fruit soften and absorb the sherry.

2 Sift the flour, cinnamon, spice and salt together. Lightly beat the eggs.

3 Cream the butter or margarine, sugar and treacle together until paler and creamy. Gradually beat in the eggs, alternately adding the sifted flour in batches until it is well mixed.

4 Stir in the soaked fruits with any liquid from the bowl until evenly mixed. Spoon into the prepared tin and bake for 1¹/₂ hours in the centre of the oven.

5 Reduce the heat to 150°C/300°F/gas mark 2 and cook for a further 2 hours. If the cake begins to darken too quickly after the first hour, reduce the heat earlier.

6 Push a metal skewer into the middle of the cake to check that it is cooked. Leave to cool in the tin.

7 When cold, turn the cake out carefully. Overwrap thoroughly in double greaseproof paper. Then wrap in foil and store in a cool place.

8 Remove the greaseproof paper and pierce the cake with a fine metal skewer all over. Spoon a little brandy over the cake, allowing it to soak into the pierced holes.

Feeding a fruit cake with brandy
• To feed your cake with brandy, rum or whisky during storage, unwrap and prick the top several times with a fine skewer. Spoon over 2-3tbsp spirit, leave to soak in well before re-wrapping and storing. Repeat 2-3 times at weekly intervals.

Golden Fruit Cake

This light golden fruit cake can be decorated within weeks of baking. Using the lighter fruits, such as pineapple, apricot, ginger and sultanas, and soaking them well with fruit juice and rum, makes a cake that is wonderfully rich and moist but in a lighter and fruitier way compared to a traditional dark fruit cake. It's a matter of taste really!

Makes one 20cm (8in) round or 18cm (7in) square cake

250g (9oz) mixed glacé cherries, glacé pineapple, ready-to-eat dried apricots, candied peel and/or crystallised ginger
200g (7oz) sultanas
200g (7oz) raisins
finely grated zest and juice of 1 small orange
finely grated zest of 1 small lemon
2-3tbsp sherry, brandy or rum
250g (9oz) butter or margarine, softened
250g (9oz) caster sugar
4 eggs
300g (11oz) plain flour, sifted
2tsp ground mixed spice
1½ tsp baking powder

1 In a large bowl mix together all the fruit, zest, juice and sherry, brandy or rum. Cover and set aside in a cold place for several hours or overnight.

2 Prepare a 20cm (8in) round or 18cm (7in) square tin (page 11). Preheat the oven to 160ºC/325ºF/gas mark 3. Cream the butter or margarine and sugar together in a large bowl until light and fluffy.

3 Beat the eggs together, then gradually stir them into the creamed mixture, adding the flour, mixed spice and baking powder in batches alternately with egg.

4 Gently stir in the soaked fruit and any juices to make a fairly soft mixture. Spoon into the prepared tin.

5 Smooth the top of the mixture and bake for 1½ hours, then reduce the heat to 150ºC/300ºF/gas mark 2 and bake for a further 1 hour. Check that the cake is cooked through. Cool in the tin.

6 Remove from the tin when cold and wrap in double-thick greaseproof paper, then foil. Store in an airtight tin until ready to decorate.

To Test if Fruit Cake is Cooked

- The cake should look slightly shrunk away from the sides of the tin. Press the top to check if it is firm.
- Push a clean metal skewer into the centre of the cake, if it comes out with sticky mixture on it, return the cake to the oven.
- A fruit cake that is not fully cooked will definitely make a noise – a slight humming.

Fruit and nut topping

For a quick fruit cake decoration, simply arrange glacé fruits and whole nuts neatly on top of the matured cake and brush with golden syrup or honey.

Guide to Proportions for Tin Sizes (fruit cakes)

Ingredients	15cm (6in) round 13cm (5in) square	20cm (8in) round 18cm (7in) square	25cm (10in) round 23cm (9in) square	30cm (12in) round 28cm (11in) square

Dark Rich Fruit Cake

Ingredients	15cm (6in) round / 13cm (5in) square	20cm (8in) round / 18cm (7in) square	25cm (10in) round / 23cm (9in) square	30cm (12in) round / 28cm (11in) square
Mixed dried fruit	450g (1lb)	850g (1lb 14oz)	1.5kg (3 1/2lb)	2.25kg (5lb)
Glacé cherries	75g (3oz)	110g (4oz)	175g (6oz)	350g (12oz)
Flaked almonds or chopped nuts	50g (2oz)	75g (3oz)	150g (5oz)	225g (8oz)
Grated zest	1/2 lemon and 1/2 orange	1 lemon and 1 orange	1 lemon and 1 1/2 small oranges	1 1/2 lemons and 1 1/2 oranges
Orange juice	2tbsp	3tbsp	4tbsp	6tbsp
Sherry, brandy or rum	2tbsp	3tbsp	4tbsp	6tbsp
Plain flour	150g (5oz)	250g (9oz)	450g (1lb)	675g (1 1/2lb)
Ground cinnamon	1/2tsp	1tsp	1 1/2tsp	2tsp
Ground mixed spice	1tsp	1 1/2 tsp	2tsp	2 1/2tsp
Salt	1/2tsp	1tsp	1 1/2tsp	2tsp
Eggs	3	4	6	9
Butter or margarine	140g (4 1/2oz)	200g (7oz)	400g (14oz)	625g (1lb 6oz)
Soft dark brown sugar	140g (4 1/2oz)	200g (7oz)	400g (14oz)	625g (1lb 6oz)
Treacle or syrup	1/2 tbsp	1tbsp	1 1/2 tbsp	2tbsp
Baking time	**1 1/2–2 hours**	**3–3 1/4 hours**	**4 hours**	**5–5 1/4 hours**

Golden Fruit Cake

Ingredients	15cm (6in) round / 13cm (5in) square	20cm (8in) round / 18cm (7in) square	25cm (10in) round / 23cm (9in) square	30cm (12in) round / 28cm (11in) square
Mixed candied or glacé fruits: pineapple, cherries, apricots, mango, ginger, peel	110g (4oz)	250g (9oz)	450g (1lb)	600g (1lb 5oz)
Mixed sultanas and raisins	250g (9oz)	400g (14oz)	1kg (2 1/4lb)	1.5kg (3 1/4lb)
Grated zest and juice of	1/2 orange	1 orange	1 1/2 orange	2 oranges
Sherry, brandy or liqueur	2tbsp	3tbsp	5tbsp	7-8tbsp
Butter or margarine	150g (5oz)	250g (9oz)	575g (1 1/4lb)	800g (1lb 12oz)
Soft light brown sugar	150g (5oz)	250g (9oz)	575g (1 1/4lb)	800g (1lb 12oz)
Eggs	2	4	6	10
Plain flour	175g (6oz)	300g (11oz)	575g (1 1/4lb)	900g (2lb)
Salt	1/2tsp	1tsp	1 1/2tsp	2tsp
Ground mixed spice	1tsp	2tsp	4tsp	6tsp
Baking powder	1tsp	2tsp	3 1/2tsp	5tsp
Baking time	**2 hours**	**2 1/2–3hours**	**3 3/4–4hours**	**5 hours**

Icings and Frostings

Icings, frostings and fillings can transform a plain cake into a quick and simple teatime treat or a glamorous creation that keeps moist and delicious for longer. If you are making an impressive gâteau for a special occasion it can be prepared well in advance, as some of these mixtures will keep well for 3-4 days, or more.

Butter Icing

This popular icing, sometimes called butter cream, gives a creamy rich finish. It can be flavoured and coloured in numerous ways. It is very easy to make and work with as its rich and creamy texture quickly covers any surface and fills any gap. Turn a simple sponge into an elegant gâteau in minutes by swirling butter icing delicately around the sides and piping it stylishly over the top.

1 Place the butter in a mixing bowl and beat until pale and fluffy. Gradually beat in the icing sugar and lemon juice or vanilla. Beat in 1tbsp hot (boiled but not boiling) water, beating all the time to give a soft-peak consistency.

2 Add any chosen flavourings, with extra icing sugar as necessary to retain the right consistency. Use immediately or cover and chill until required. Bring the butter icing back to room temperature before use.

Sufficient to fill and top two 20cm (8in) sponge cakes

110g (4oz) unsalted butter, softened
250g (9oz) icing sugar, sifted
2tsp lemon juice or a few drops of vanilla essence

Variations
• Add 1tbsp cocoa powder blended with 1tbsp hot water.
• Add 2tsp instant coffee blended with 1tsp boiling water.
• Add 2tsp finely grated zest of lemon, orange or lime.

Simple Finishes for Butter Icing

The butter icing should be firm enough to give a good shape but soft enough to spread easily. Simply swirling it over the top or around the sides of a cake always looks good. You can create many effects by using a fork, serrated comb, ruler or a palette knife.

1 Completely cover the cake with icing. Use a flat ruler to flatten and smooth the top, or use the serrated edge to give a neat lined effect before adding the final decorations.

2 If you are not decorating the top and need a more stylish finish, pull a wide fork through the icing in two different directions to make a pronounced square or angular pattern.

3 The side can be marked quickly with a small- to medium-sized palette knife. Place the clean and dry blade flat upright against the icing. Press gently to smooth the icing and create a luscious effect. Slide the knife upwards and remove gently. Do not pull it away too sharply.

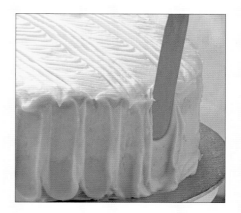

Meringue Butter Icing

Sufficient to coat two 20cm (8in) sponge cakes

(topping and coating)

75g (3oz) sugar
4½ tbsp water
3 egg whites
175g (6oz) unsalted butter, softened
few drops of vanilla essence

Variations

• For a rich chocolate butter icing, melt and slightly cool 75g (3oz) good dark chocolate. Work it into the meringue butter icing after the butter. This becomes quite stiff on cooling, so spread or pipe before it cools too much.
• Flavourings for butter icing (previous page) can be used in meringue butter icing.

This richer and glossier version of butter icing is perfect for special occasion cakes and gâteau. It has a finer, lighter flavour than standard butter icing. It keeps really well in a container in the refrigerator and also on the cake.

1 Dissolve the sugar in the water in a small clean saucepan and then bring to the boil. Boil the sugar syrup to a temperature of 115°C/239°F.

2 Whisk the egg whites in a large heatproof bowl until they stand in soft peaks. Place over a pan of gently simmering water and whisk in the syrup. Continue whisking until the mixture is thick and glossy.

3 Cream the butter until it is soft. Using an electric whisk, gradually incorporate the butter into the meringue until the icing is firm and glossy. Flavour with a little vanilla. Cover with cling film and leave to cool before spreading or piping.

Glacé Icing

There is nothing simpler and quicker to make and use than a glacé icing. It can be coloured and flavoured, spread, drizzled and feathered, but not piped into sophisticated designs. Youngsters can make this icing easily by themselves. Getting the consistency right is important or the icing can run all over the place.

Sufficient to coat 12 small cakes

110g (4oz) icing sugar
1-2tbsp water

1 Sift the sugar into a small bowl and add 1tbsp water. Mix until the water is worked in. Then add more water by ¼ teaspoon at a time. When blended but thick, beat hard to remove any lumps. Then work in drops of water for the consistency you need.

2 Add flavouring and colouring to taste and use immediately. If not using the icing immediately, cover closely with cling film as the surface will very quickly crust over and the icing with then go lumpy when stirred.

Icing small cakes

Place the fairy cakes on a wire rack. Place the rack on a board or over greaseproof paper to catch any drips. Using a teaspoon, spoon icing into the centre of each cake, leave it to settle for a few seconds, then tap the edge of the cake rack very gently to help the icing flow to its own smooth level.

Feather icing

Make up a small quantity of a contrasting colour of icing. Alternatively, use melted chocolate or jam (sieved). Spoon a little into a small paper piping bag without a nozzle. Snip off the end to make a small hole and pipe lines or circles on the wet white icing. Use a skewer or cocktail stick to pull lines through the two colours to give the feathered effect.

American Frosting

Used for many traditional American cakes, such as carrot cake or angel cake, this frosting peaks wonderfully and has a mallowy texture with a slight crust when cold. It takes only 8-10 minutes to make but is best whisked until cool before using. On an uncut cake it keeps well for several days.

Sufficient to cover top and sides of a 23cm (9in) cake

150g (5oz) caster sugar
1tbsp water
1tbsp golden syrup
1 large egg white

1 Mix all the ingredients together in a large clean heatproof bowl. Place over a saucepan of simmering water. Whisk lightly until the sugar has dissolved.

2 Whisk hard for several minutes, until the mixture forms stiff peaks. Remove from the heat and continue whisking until the frosting cools.

3 Spread the frosting generously over the top and sides of the cake.

4 Make peaks or attractive swirls, and leave until cold, by which time the frosting will have acquired a slightly crisp surface.

Italian Meringue

Italian meringue is a very stable mixture and it is often used as a frosting. The egg whites are whisked with syrup instead of sugar. Like American Frosting, it also forms a slight crust when cold but it remains gooey underneath.

Sufficient to cover the top and sides of a 23cm (9in) cake

175g (6oz) caster sugar
6tbsp water
2 egg whites

1 Dissolve the sugar in the water in a medium saucepan and bring to the boil. Boil until clear and syrupy.

2 Whisk the egg whites in a large heatproof bowl over a saucepan of simmering water until they are stiff.

3 Gradually pour in the hot syrup in a slow trickle, whisking hard all the time. Continue whisking until the meringue is very stiff and glossy. Remove from the heat and keep whisking until the mixture is cool.

4 Use immediately or cover with cling film and keep in a cool place (not the refrigerator) for 2-3 days.

Marzipan

Also known as almond paste, marzipan is a pliable mixture of ground almonds, icing sugar, egg and lemon juice. It is used as a base coat for a madeira or rich fruit cake to prevent the oils from the cake seeping out into the white icing. Marzipan provides a smooth surface for icing and it improves the keeping qualities of a cake. You do not have to use marzipan – or you could simply apply a very thin layer.

Bought marzipan is available natural, uncoloured and known as white marzipan, or as egg yellow marzipan. Home-made is always much paler than bought. Marzipan can be coloured with food colours and moulded into different shapes for decoration. Both shapes and the covered cake need 10-12 hours to dry out and firm up.

Marzipan Tips

• Keep marzipan cool and do not knead too much as it can become oily.
• When rolling out, use a little sifted icing sugar to prevent sticking. Do not add other flours, such as cornflour, as they ferment during storage.
• Home-made marzipan will keep in the refrigerator for 2-3 months, or it can be frozen for up to a year.
• Leftover marzipan can be grated and added to crumble toppings or used to flavour cakes and puddings.
• A Simnel cake has a layer of marzipan placed in the middle of the mixture before baking.
• For good keeping qualities, a fruit cake must be well fitted on the board and the marzipan should create a complete airtight seal before you begin icing.

Health Concerns

If you make cakes for gifts or for public occasions or are worried about the use of raw egg in marzipan or royal icing, buy dried egg products instead. These ingredients have been heat treated to ensure they are safe. Alternatively, buy marzipan or icing. To ensure it keeps well, boil apricot glaze before use.

Marzipan

Makes about 475g (1lb)
Sufficient to cover top and sides of one 20cm (8in) round or 18cm (7in) square cake

225g (8oz) ground almonds
110g (4oz) caster sugar
110g (4oz) icing sugar, sifted
1 egg, lightly beaten
1tbsp lemon juice

1 Mix the almonds, caster and icing sugars in a bowl. Work in the egg and lemon juice until the mixture is fairly stiff.

2 Turn out onto a lightly sugared work surface and knead gently for a few minutes, until really smooth.

3 Wrap tightly in cling film or place in a polythene bag until required.

Apricot Glaze

Apricot glaze is used to keep the marzipan in place. Warm 5-6tbsp apricot jam with 2tbsp water in a small saucepan. Bring to the boil, stirring, and then sieve the jam to remove lumps of fruit. Cool slightly.

Covering a Cake with Marzipan

There are two ways to marzipan a cake. Either the all-in-one method, which is ideal for round cakes and as a base for sugar paste, or by covering the top and sides separately. The latter gives a cake with squarer edges and is used as a base for royal icing.

If necessary, trim off any slight dome of mixture to flatten the top of the cake. Brush with a little apricot glaze and invert the cake onto a board. This provides a flat surface to work on. Fill any large holes, or gaps around the base of the cake with pieces or strips of marzipan, smoothing them in place. Brush the cake all over with apricot glaze.

All-in-one Method

1 Measure the diameter of the cake. Add double the depth of the side and at least 2.5cm (1in) extra. Roll out the marzipan on a surface lightly dusted with sifted icing sugar to a circle or square the size you have calculated.

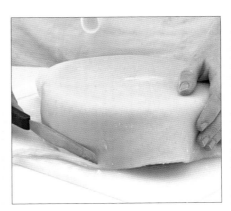

2 To lift the marzipan, roll it loosely over the rolling pin, then lift it over the cake and unroll it in place.

3 Gently ease the marzipan down the sides pressing lightly so it sticks. Smooth out the curves and around the corners of a square cake. With a sharp knife cut away the excess and neaten the base edges with a palette knife.

Two-stage Method

1 Roll out half the marzipan and cut a circle, or square, to fit the top of the cake. Gently place this on top, easing it exactly to the edges and smooth over.

2 Roll out the rest of the marzipan and cut four side pieces measured to the height and length of the cake sides. Attach each piece individually, carefully trimming off the excess at the corners. Gently smooth over the joins. Brush each section of cake with apricot glaze when necessary, rather than glazing the entire cake, so you can hold the uncoated sides while you work.

3 For a round cake, cut a strip of paste to fit the height of the cake (including the top covering of marzipan) and long enough to fit the circumference. Carefully roll this up from the short side.

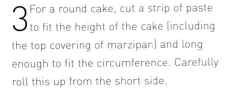

4 Place the marzipan roll against the side of the cake and unroll it carefully while turning the board. Press it gently into position as you turn. Then trim and seal the joins neatly.

Royal Icing

Royal icing is nearly always the choice for very special formal cakes. It gives an elegant bright-white covering and it can be used in very simple or very complex ways. Antique Victorian and Edwardian designs show the ultimate use of piped decoration but even simple, minimal icing can give a very elegant modern result.

Make royal icing using raw ingredients or you can buy commercially prepared powder mixes. These mixes include precise proportions of albumen (egg white), glucose or glycerine necessary for making icing for different tasks. For example, glycerine is added to give a coating icing that stays soft for cutting, while run-out icing needs sufficient albumen for it to become dry and hard, but contains no glycerine.

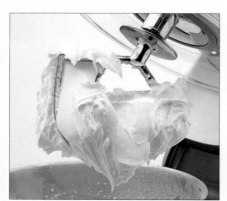

Royal Icing

Makes sufficient to coat top and sides of a 20cm (8in) round or 18cm (7in) square cake

2 egg whites or 40g (1¹/₂ oz) albumen powder
1tbsp lemon juice
2tsp glycerine (use only for coating icing)
450g (1lb) icing sugar, sifted twice

1 Lightly whisk the egg whites, lemon juice and glycerine (if using) in a large bowl. If using albumen powder, make it up according to the packet instructions. Gradually work in the sifted icing sugar.

2 Continue beating until the icing is stiff, smooth and glossy. For flat coating, the icing should stand in soft peaks, so when you lift the spoon out of the bowl the icing stands in a peak with a gentle curve.

3 Cover the bowl of icing with a clean damp tea towel or cling film and leave for about 1 hour before using to allow any air bubbles to disperse.

Flat Icing a Round Cake

When flat icing a cake, you will achieve the best results by giving the top and sides 2-3 coats, allowing each coat to dry well before adding the next. Coat the top and side in separate stages, allowing them to dry between coats. Speed things up by storing the cake in an airy, dry place under a lamp if possible. Before you move on to the next stage, gently scrape off any lumps or snags with a scalpel and fill any holes with soft icing.

1 To coat the top, place 2-3 tablespoons of icing in the middle and gently spread it over with a palette knife. Do this using a flat paddling movement. The top of the cake should be even covered.

Royal Icing Tips
- Royal icing can be made in a food mixer but not a food processor.
- Royal icing benefits from being left to rest for at least 1 hour so any air bubbles can disperse.
- Keep the icing well covered with cling film or a damp cloth at all times to prevent it from drying out before you have finished using it.
- Use a turntable to lift the cake to a comfortable working height and to turn it easily while you work.
- Always let one coating become totally dry before repairing it or applying another coat.

2 Draw a straight edge or clean icing ruler firmly and smoothly across the top of the cake. Hold the ruler at an angle of about 45 degrees. Do this in one movement – if you stop you will have a ridge. If necessary, repeat the whole process, but remember that the next two layers will cover up any problems. Set aside until firm.

3 To coat the side, spread the icing roughly around the cake with a palette knife, making sure all the marzipan is evenly covered.

4 Use a plain-edged cake scraper and start at the opposite side of the cake, furthest away from you. Hold the turntable with the left hand and the scraper in the right hand. The scraper should be vertical and at an angle of about 45 degrees. Turn the cake steadily in one continuous movement while scraping the icing firmly. When both hands meet, carefully slide the left hand out of the way and pull the scraper towards you. This can be repeated, but unless the coat is really uneven it will be improved when the next coating is applied. Set aside until firm.

5 When the icing has dried, smooth any rough edges carefully. Gently scrape off any rough ridges and then coat top and sides again.

6 Once you are happy with the flat icing, cover the board in a similar way to the sides. Spread a thin coat first with a palette knife, then gently drag the scraper over the board, pulling it towards you at the end to avoid creating a ridge.

Flat Icing a Square Cake

1 Coat the top in exactly the same way as for a round cake.

2 For the sides, coat lightly all over as for a round cake. Then smooth one side at a time with the same angled and firm action. Finish at the corner by bringing the scraper off the cake towards you. Start the next side by joining up with the previous edge and continue this way around all four sides. Set aside until firm. Apply second and third coats in similar stages.

Sugar Paste Tips

• Always keep sugar paste covered when you are not working with it. It quickly forms a crust that can cause lumps. If it does dry out, cut off any hard edges, then knead it again gently inside a plastic bag.
• Keep a clean pastry brush handy to brush away any cake or dry paste crumbs that might ruin your sugar paste.
• Don't let sugar paste get too warm when handling it or it becomes difficult to roll out and handle.
• Always use sifted icing sugar to dust the surface and rolling pin as any small lumps will spoil the sugar paste. Use cornflour for very fine designs in flower paste or pastillage.
• The finished coat of sugar paste can be gently polished with a special smooth plastic smoother or with a small lump of leftover paste wrapped in a polythene bag. Dust with a little icing sugar.

Sugar Paste

Sugar paste is also known as ready-to-roll icing, or it may sometimes be called fondant. It is easy to use, very forgiving and great fun for everyone to use. Sugar paste gives a professional finish with little effort. A sugar paste covering will keep a cake fresher for longer than, for example, butter icing. Most larger supermarkets sell sugar paste and specialist cake decorating suppliers have a selection of pastes.

Cakes can be wonderfully colourful and theme cakes are great fun to prepare. For the more complex designs, plaques and lace or filigree work, there are other sugar pastes that can be made at home. These are easy to prepare if you have a mixer, but you can also buy prepared powders or pastes from specialist shops. The harder pastes used for modelling and making flowers are not intended to be eaten – they do not contain inedible ingredients but they set to a hard, unpalatable finish. Decorations made from these pastes will keep indefinitely if stored in an airtight container in a cool dry place.

Modelling paste: This is stronger than standard sugar paste, yet very pliable for making models, animals and larger shapes. It contains gum tragacanth, an ingredient that helps to give the paste strength.

Flower paste: Also known as petal or gum paste, this also contains gum tragacanth, as well as a little white vegetable fat. This can be rolled and moulded thinly to make delicate decorations, flowers and foliage.

Pastillage: This dries rock hard. It is ideal for intricate, tall or arched designs.

Sugar Paste

1 egg white or 20g (³/₄oz) albumen powder
2tbsp liquid glucose, warmed
450g (1lb) icing sugar, sifted

Sufficient to cover top and sides of a 20cm (8in) round or 18cm (7in) square cake

1 Place the egg white in a mixing bowl. Alternatively, make up the albumen as directed on the packet. Lightly beat in the liquid glucose. Gradually work in the icing sugar with a wooden spoon until it begins to form a paste.

2 Knead the paste gently into a ball with your fingertips. Turn onto a clean dry surface and knead well until smooth. Dust the surface with sifted icing sugar if the paste sticks, and work in extra icing sugar if it is too sticky.

3 If you are not using it immediately, wrap the paste tightly in cling film and store in a cool place or in the refrigerator.

Covering a Round Cake with Sugar Paste

A sponge or fruit cake can be covered directly, without a marzipan layer, as long as the surface is flat and free from loose crumbs. Any lumps will show through the sugar paste.

1 Cover a sponge cake with a light coating of apricot glaze (page 26) or butter icing. Brush a fruit cake with boiled water or clear alcohol such as gin or vodka.

2 Measure from the base of one side of the cake, over the top and down to the base on the other side. Knead the paste briefly to warm and soften it, then roll out on a sugar-dusted surface, into a circle 2.5-5cm (1-2in) larger than the total top and sides measurement.

3 Roll the paste loosely over the rolling pin and lift it carefully over the cake. Gently unroll it and smooth the paste down the sides. Trim the excess from the bottom edge.

4 For a polished result, smooth the surface with a plastic smoother, or use a small lump of extra paste wrapped in a small plastic bag.

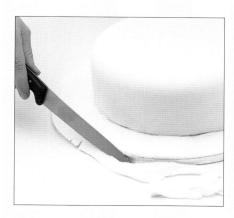

5 To cover the board, roll out a band of paste the same width and circumference as the exposed board. Roll this up loosely. Brush the board with a little boiled water or alcohol, then carefully unwrap the paste on to it. Trim and seal the paste at the join and then trim the edge around the board.

Covering a Square Cake with Sugar Paste

1 Measure from the base of one side of the cake, over the top and down to the base on the other side. Roll out the paste large enough to cut out a square of paste 2.5-5cm (1-2in) larger than this measurement. Carefully roll the paste loosely on the pin, and then lift it over the prepared cake and unroll in position.

2 Smooth the paste from the centre out to the corners. Lift the excess paste at the corners as you smooth it on the cake and down the sides.

3 Smooth the paste well. Trim the excess paste from the edges and then cover the board, as above, if you wish.

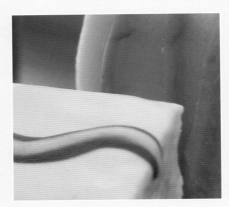

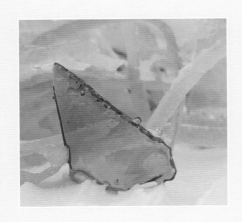

Decorating with Style

The fun part of making a cake is the decorating and finishing. Seeing your idea or design come to fruition, and hearing the appreciation of family and friends, is what it's all about. Whether you have spent a couple of hours or a couple of days creating the cake, the end result is what matters.

Map the design fully before you start so that you can assemble colours, tools, trimmings and any specialist items. If you haven't used a technique before, take time to try it out before working on the cake. Allow for breakages by making extra decorations. Plan your work in stages, working backward from the day the cake is required to the baking day.

Drying time is among the most important stages – for marzipan to harden, icing to set, and sugar paste to firm up. Any delicate decorations, flowers and cut-outs will need at least 1-2 days to dry before they can be assembled on the final cake. Do not forget to plan for setting and drying or you may run out of time.

Decorating with Royal Icing

Royal icing was created for royal occasions and often used for very intricate designs far too complex and time consuming for the majority of today's requirements. However, a traditional occasion, for example a wedding, calls for something really special by way of a decorated cake, and many people like the royal icing finish. Royal icing more versatile than it first appears to be. It can be used for delicate, simple designs that are modern and do not require great skill or too much practice. Getting the consistency right for piping royal icing is vital, particularly if you are decorating several cakes or tiers – as your wrists will ache if the icing is too stiff.

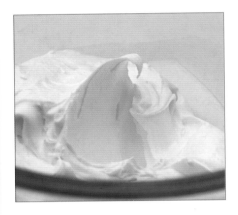

Soft Peak

This is the basic consistency for flat icing a marzipan-covered cake. The icing should hold a peak that just falls over slightly at the tip.

Full or Firm Peak

Suitable for most piping tasks. The icing peaks stay firm and sharp. Don't make it too firm or it will be difficult to pipe.

Very Firm Peak

This is the ideal consistency for a Christmas snow scene. Keep working in more icing sugar until it stands up in stiff, short sharp peaks.

Run-out Icing

For outlining a template the icing needs to be almost as stiff as soft peak – maybe a touch softer.

Flooding Consistency

To 'flood' a shape, the icing needs to be much looser. To test, spoon a little into a bowl and the lines and edges of any peaks should fade within 8 seconds.

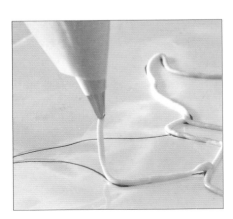

To Make and Fill a Piping Bag

You can never have too many small piping bags. Even though you may buy ready made bags, there will be occasions when you need to make one.

1 Start with a square of waxed paper approximately 25cm (10in) square. Fold in half into two triangles. Crease from the middle of the long side to the point.

2 Holding the points opposite the long side with one hand, roll the left corner over to line up with them. Do the same with the other corner so it wraps around making a cone with all the points neatly together.

3 Shuffle the points until they meet neatly. Ensure the cone has a good shape, with a firm point at the bottom.

4 Fold over and secure the points you are holding with tape or a staple clip. If you are using a nozzle, snip a little off the tip of the bag and insert the nozzle.

5 Only half fill with icing. Then fold over the top to enclose the icing.

6 Fold the corners firmly in towards the middle and fold the top over again. Gently squeeze the icing down into the nozzle. If you are not using a nozzle, cut off a tiny point from the tip of the piping bag equivalent to the size of the nozzle you need.

Nozzles
- For fine lines use a small plain nozzle, no. 1 or 2.
- For small rosettes, stars or shells use a no. 5, 7, 9 or 11.
- For ropes use a 42, 43 or 44.

Piping

Hold the bag in one hand, between thumb and fingers, so that the thumb can be used to push the icing down the bag. Use the other hand as a support. Firmly, but with even pressure, push the icing down the bag, trying not to squeeze the whole lot with your hand.

To pipe lines: Touch the surface with the nozzle to attach the icing first. Start to squeeze as you lift up and slowly pull backwards. Let the icing hang without pulling so that you can position the line or shape. Stop applying pressure when you see the end of the line. Lower the nozzle down to touch the surface and seal the line in place. Lift off the nozzle.

To pipe a snail trail: This is a delicate line with small regular dots. It looks pretty and more modern than many other designs. Start by piping a very small ball, release pressure and drag a short piped line. Then apply pressure to pipe another small ball. Continue for the required length.

To work cornelli or filigree piping: This looks very effective and can cover large areas quickly. You have to be very consistent with the pressure and size of line for this to look good. The design consists of m's and w's run on together without stopping. These two letters create a soft-flowing design to fill any area. Practise first.

To pipe balls: Touch the surface and pipe without moving until the icing forms the size of ball you require. Then release the pressure before lifting up the nozzle to avoid leaving a long peak. The size of the ball is dictated by the length of time you pipe on the spot.

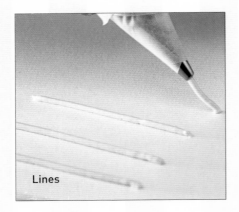
Lines

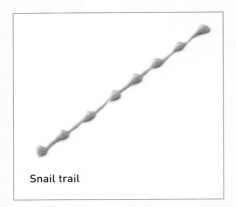
Snail trail

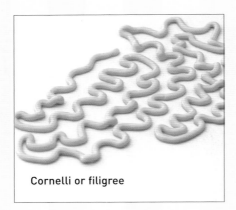
Cornelli or filigree

Stars

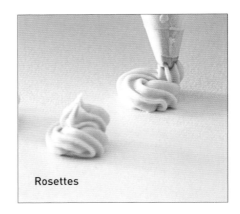
Rosettes

Balls

Shells

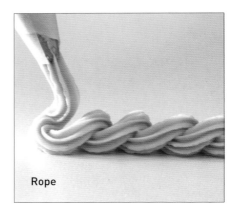
Rope

To pipe stars: Using a star nozzle, hold the bag vertical and steady on the surface. Apply pressure without moving the bag. Pull up sharply to make a small or large point. Use a larger nozzle and more pressure for a large star.

To pipe a rosette: Using a star nozzle, hold the bag vertical, touch the surface and squeeze out the beginning of a shell shape. At the same time, rotate the bag in a very small circle and raise it. Pull up and release pressure to leave a pointed tip.

To pipe shells: Touch the nozzle down on the surface, squeeze at an angle of 45º until sufficient icing comes out. Release the pressure and point the nozzle down to cut off the icing, at the same time, pull back to make a very slight tail. Start the next shell immediately on this tail to link the shells.

To pipe a rope: Begin by piping a rosette but do not finish off. Continue rotating the bag, at the same time as moving it along in a line.

To pipe a small flower: Use a flat petal tube (no. 57). Use a little icing to attach a small piece of greaseproof paper to a flower nail. Hold the tube flat with its wide end in the centre and squeeze out a petal shape at the same time twisting the flower nail in a full circle. Pipe another petal partly over the first in the same way. Repeat. Finally pipe one petal in the opposite direction to fill the gap. Pipe yellow dots in the centre and leave to set.

Royal Icing Run-outs

A run-out is a hard icing shape. The outline is piped and the centre filled in or 'flooded' with softened royal icing. Run-outs have to set hard, so glycerine must not be used. If different colours are used, it is important to ensure that one area has set and formed a dry skin before piping adjoining areas.

Trace the design on greaseproof paper. Cover with silicone paper, securing it in place with a little icing. Using run-out consistency icing, pipe over the design outline and any inner lines. Leave to dry – place under a warm lamp to speed up the drying time. Fill the outline with softer, flooding-consistency icing. Leave for up to 24 hours to dry completely. Use a palette knife to lift the run-out off the paper. Attach to the cake with a little icing.

To create run-outs with a three-dimensional effect, pipe and fill separate sections. Assemble the sections at different angles or levels directly on the surface of the cake, supporting each piece with soft paper or a corner of sponge until firm.

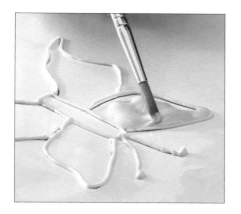

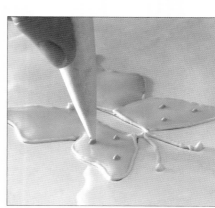

Decorating with Sugar Paste

Sugar paste is a versatile and forgiving medium to work with, especially for fun designs and theme cakes. Be as adventurous or creative as you dare because you can re-model a shape – whether it's a teddy bear or a fine rose – until you get it right. Effects like frills and folds, pleats and patterns, ribbons and bows are easily made using cutters, crimpers and specialist modelling tools available. Colours can be used to shade and marble the paste, or to dust, paint and sponge on. Once finished, sugar paste does not take long to dry, so the cake can be assembled in a day or two.

Cut-out Shapes

All sorts of flat shapes can be cut out of sugar paste. Letters, numbers, flowers or animals – there are endless cutters, or for a specific design, draw a template and cut it out in cardboard or firm paper. Once the shapes are cut, leave them on a board to dry out for 1-2 hours. Cut-outs can be given a three-dimensional effect by cutting two sizes of the same design and sticking them together. Alternatively, gently bend the shape over soft paper or a corner of sponge and leave until dry. Paint or colour shapes as required.

Colouring Carefully

Sugar paste takes colour easily but some colours are stronger than others. When buying colours, remember that pastes and powders are easier to work with than liquids.

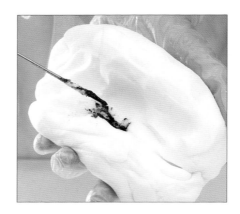

• Take a small amount of sugar paste and use a cocktail stick to add the colour drop by drop, kneading in each addition until you achieve the desired colour. Cover and set aside until required.

• There are two ways to marble paste. Either avoid working in the colour thoroughly or make up batches of paste in two or more colours and then gently knead the different pastes together to achieve the required effect.

• For topping a cake, roll out and use the paste immediately and allow it to dry before adding decorations.

Delicate Designs

Pastillage and flower paste are used to make very delicate flowers or fine shapes and for designs that need to be attached to wire. Roll out the pastillage on a surface lightly dusted with cornflour and cut out using a template and a damp knife. If using a fine patchwork template, grease the edges with a little white fat to help the paste come off the template easily. Allow to dry for about 2 hours on a surface lightly dusted with cornflour. Turn over and dry for a further 2 hours or until dry – larger or thicker pieces may need longer. Paint or decorate when absolutely dry. Assemble shapes or attach plaques with royal icing. Handle with care, as they are very fragile. Make more shapes than you will need to allow for breakages.

Roping and Plaiting

Rolling and twisting one, two or more colours of sugar paste or marzipan together produces exciting and varied rope effects.

Straight-edged rope: Roll the chosen colours out to the same thickness and cut even strips. Twist them together gently and evenly. For cake edging, attach strips to the dampened cake or board as you twist them so there is minimal movement of the rope.

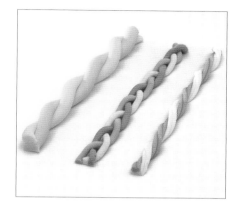

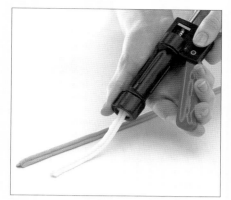

Rounded roping or plaiting: Roll out the colours into long thin sausage shapes of the same length and thickness. Twist or plait colours together. Roll the rope together gently if you need to make it longer or want a flattened effect.

Note: For speed and ease use a sugar paste gun.

Colouring and Moulding Tips
- Use fine plastic gloves when kneading in strong colours, such as black or Christmas green.
- Keep a tiny piece of coloured paste as reference in case you need to match up colours later.
- Wrap in cling film or place in a polythene bag immediately.
- Work delicate items between pieces of polythene or cling film.

Flowers

Beautiful flowers and blossoms can be made using pastillage, flower paste or marzipan. Use a flower cutter with a two-piece rubber mould to create the final shape and veining. Alternatively, use a simple blossom cutter with a plunger, and finish the blossoms by hand.

1 Roll out the paste quite thinly. When you are experienced you can use pastillage or flower paste very thinly to produce delicate results.

2 Cut out the flower or blossom shapes and press them between rubber moulds lightly dusted with cornflour. Tease the blooms out onto a gently curved surface so that they bend and curl like real flowers.

3 Leave the flowers to dry for several hours. To paint them, use a tiny brush dipped in edible colour and catch the edges of the petals or brush fine lines on the petals. Attach silver or pearl centres with a drop of royal icing. Dust with flower colours, silver or pearl dusting powders.

Plunger Cutter: Alternatively, cut out blossoms with a plunger cutter. These may be small or very tiny. Using a cocktail stick or frilling tool, indent the middle of the blossom curve to give a petal effect.

Frilly Petals: For a floppy petal effect, gently run over the edges of each petal with a cocktail stick until it is frilled up.

Frills and Folds

Simple frills can be used to edge a cake or board. The same technique can be used to finish the centres of flowers or petal edges.

Frilled strip: Roll out a strip of paste or marzipan on a lightly sugared board. Roll a cocktail stick or friller tool firmly along one edge. Keep moving so that the paste does not stick to the board. Lift the frill carefully to put it in place. Or roll up into a tight carnation-style flower head. For a different effect fold or pleat the edge of the paste by pinching gently.

Frilled circle: Cut out a circle of paste. Roll a cocktail stick or friller tool at intervals around the edge.

Circular frill: Frill a circle of paste as above, then stamp out the middle with a cutter. A small circular frill can be applied to a figure model as a skirt.

Larger circular frills can be used as edging or top decoration on cakes.

Frilled or pleated covered board: Roll a cocktail stick over the paste covering a board to give a frilled or pleated effect.

Using Simple Tools

A crimper or embossing tool is quick and easy to use. The choice is huge. The paste or marzipan must be soft for this technique.

Embossing tools: Dip the tool into icing sugar to prevent the paste from sticking. Gently press the tool into the paste to make regular or random patterns to suit your design. Dust or paint colour over immediately and leave to dry.

Crimping tools: For top and bottom edges of a cake or a board edge, pinch the crimper on the paste so that it is about 5-7mm ($1/4 - 1/3$in) thick.

Decorating with Chocolate

Chocolate is popular for all types of cakes, including more formal occasions such as weddings. It is generally easy to work with for both simple and stunning effects.

Mixed with butter, sugar or cream in varying proportions, melted chocolate makes a variety of excellent coatings and fillings. Dark, milk or white chocolate can all be used. Two different types of result can be achieved by working with the chocolate either warm or when cold and set. For the best flavour, use a good-quality chocolate with a high percentage of cocoa solids.

Ganache

225g (8oz) dark, milk or white chocolate,
   broken into pieces
120ml (4floz) whipping cream
50g (2oz) unsalted butter, softened

1 Put the chocolate in a bowl. Heat the cream in a small saucepan until it is almost boiling.

2 Pour the hot cream into the chocolate, stirring until the chocolate has melted and blended with the cream.

3 While still warm, work in the butter, which should be almost runny but not translucent.

Flavouring ganache: Add any of the following before the ganache becomes firm.
- 1-2tsp finely grated orange or lemon zest
- 1/2-1tsp grated nutmeg or ground cinnamon
- 2-3tbsp brandy, whisky, Cointreau or your favourite spirit
- 1-2tbsp strong black coffee or fresh orange juice

Coating with ganache: Allow the ganache to cool and thicken slightly. Pour it all over the top of the cake in one firm swift movement. Spread the ganache gently for an even covering, or if it is still very runny, tap the cake board gently on the surface so the coating runs evenly. Leave to cool and set.

Frosting or piping with ganache: Leave until cool but not set. Beat the ganache well with a wooden spoon and it will lighten into a fluffy frosting. Spread this evenly as a filling or over the top or sides of a cake. For piping, spoon into a medium piping bag fitted with a star nozzle and pipe rosettes or roping around the cake.

Melting Chocolate

Chocolate can be melted in a bowl over hot water or in the microwave. It is important to remember a few guidelines.
- When melting chocolate in a bowl over a saucepan of hot water, the water must not boil – it should barely simmer. The base of the bowl must be higher than the water level. If the bowl sits in the water the chocolate will overheat. It will thicken, become oily and/or separate slightly – it is said to 'seize'.
- If any water or moisture (including steam) comes into contact with the chocolate it will seize as above.
- Do not stir too much until the chocolate has fully melted.
- Microwave carefully and on medium, not a higher setting, and in short bursts of 30-50 seconds. When overcooked or burnt the chocolate is useless.

Chocolate Curls

Make curls in advance, not in a last-minute rush, and store them in an airtight container in a dry place. They will keep for a few days. Do not put them in the refrigerator, as condensation will form on them when you bring them back to room temperature.

Melt about 110g (4oz) chocolate until thoroughly melted and quite smooth. Spread out in two batches on clean flat trays or boards. Marble is ideal to work on as it is cool but other smooth surfaces are also good. Spread the chocolate smoothly and evenly but not too thinly. Let it cool or leave in a cool place briefly to set. The chocolate will lose its gloss when ready. Watch the chocolate closely – when it has become too set it will be brittle and will not roll. The atmosphere and heat of the kitchen will determine how quickly it sets. Transfer it to a cooler place, if necessary, for a few minutes. You can re-melt the chocolate leftovers and repeat the process until you have sufficient curls.

Curls, caraque, cigars or rolls are made from melted chocolate using different tools.

Caraque: This is the term for long thin spiky curls. Use a large blade or spatula and pull it towards you at an acute angle over the surface of the chocolate. The chocolate will curl and roll for as long as you keep going at the same angle.

Rolls or cigars: Use a clean new paint stripper tool or scraper. Push it through the chocolate making a thicker, more even roll.

Thick curls: Use an ice cream scoop or the blunt edge of a round cutter to scrape off stubby, round curls.

Chocolate Curl Tips
• Do not work with too much chocolate. It is easier to observe and control the temperature of small quantities.
• Good-quality chocolate can be more temperamental than less-expensive products as it has a higher cocoa fat content.
• White chocolate cools and sets slower than dark chocolate.

Chocolate Leaves

Select firm fresh leaves – holly and bay are ideal as they have a well-defined shape. Wash and polish them well. Brush cooling chocolate quite thickly on the underside of each leaf. Place on greaseproof paper or foil and leave to set completely. When ready to use the leaves, gently peel the real leaves off the chocolate leaves.

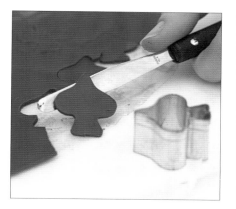

Marbling Chocolate

Marbled chocolate can be very effective for cake toppings or cut-out shapes and leaves. Melt contrasting types of chocolate separately. Pour some of one type onto a board or the top of a cake. Then add small spoonfuls of the contrasting chocolate. Use a small spoon or knife to swirl and pull the chocolates into an exciting marbled mixture. Leave to set. Marbled chocolate can also be used for cut-outs or curls.

Chocolate Shapes

Cut out shapes from thinly spread melted chocolate, prepared as for making curls. Be sure to spread the chocolate evenly and quite thinly. Carefully transfer cut-out shapes to a board or container using a palette knife and store them in a cool, dry place. Sharp, distinct and simple shapes such as squares, semi-circles, stars or teddy bears, are more successful than fussy or intricate outlines that may not stamp out easily in chocolate.

Piping Chocolate

As it cools, chocolate develops a lovely flowing texture, but do not let it get too cool. Use a small paper piping bag without a nozzle so the chocolate can be softened in the bag in the microwave if necessary, if it should become too cool. Alternatively, use a small bag with a no.1 nozzle.

Simple piped shapes can be used to decorate cakes or desserts. Draw or trace the design onto greaseproof paper. Place a sheet of cellophane over the top and pipe the chocolate over the design. Move the cellophane and pipe over the shape again. Repeat until you have made enough shapes. Cool until set.

Shapes or designs can also be piped straight onto a cake.

For a stunning result use contrasting types of chocolate. Pipe or drizzle them alternately on the design. Paper can be shaped, for example over a rolling pin, before the chocolate sets. The chocolate will then harden in a curve.

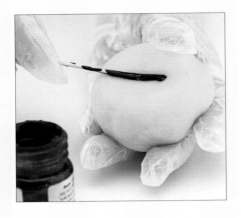

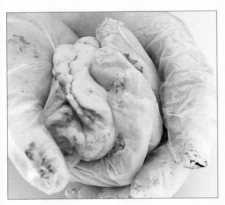

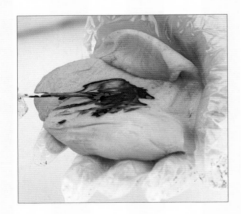

Decorating with Marzipan

Marzipan is similar to sugar paste to handle and it can be used for the same techniques. Besides covering fruit cakes it is mainly used for moulding and modelling animals, baskets, flowers and fruit.

Marzipan is more oily and moist than sugar paste therefore it needs to be left longer to dry out. A little sugar paste or pastillage can be added to marzipan to make it stronger. Marzipan can also become crumbly when dried but it can be softened by slowly kneading in a little glucose or white fat. Then allow the paste to stand for 24–48 hours before use. Your hands are the best tools for modelling, but you will also need shaped modelling tools. Remember to keep marzipan wrapped when it is not in use to prevent it from drying.

Colouring Marzipan

Use a natural marzipan base and make up light colours first. Powder and paste colours, made with alcohol or used dry are best. Water-based colours can make marzipan too moist. If you do use water-based colour, add it drop by drop with a cocktail stick or the tip of a tiny knife.
• Knead the marzipan to work in the colour. As the paste warms up in your hands, the colour will begin to blend in more evenly.
• Add colour gradually until you see how strong it is. Use fine plastic gloves when mixing in dark or strong colours.
• Chocolate marzipan, with cocoa powder kneaded in, is very successful in colour and flavour. You may want to add extra sugar or sugar syrup to large batches, to prevent the paste from drying out too much.

Marzipan Petit Fours

Marzipan can be used to make a variety of petit fours in many shapes, flavours and colours. A colourful box of marzipan fruits makes an attractive gift. They can look very realistic with a little time and patience. Use soft colours, as strong colours do not look as appetising. Dry them well to improve their keeping qualities. Simple shapes, such as carrots, apples, pears and bananas, are the best to start with.

To make carrots, colour the marzipan terracotta. Knead a small piece into a long, tapered carrot shape. With a skewer or cocktail stick, mark the characteristic indents around the carrot and mark a hole in the top for the stalks. Brush or scratch a little terracotta colour into the indents and attach 2-3 small pieces of angelica or candied lime peel for the stalks.

Marzipan Roses

The size of the finished flower is determined by the initial cone and ball of paste. When the five basic petals are in place, any number can be added to create larger or floppier blooms. To shape the petals, wear fine plastic gloves or work the marzipan between pieces of polythene or cling film with a little cornflour. This way you can create really thin petals without the past sticking.

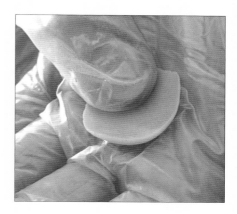

1 Mould a cone of paste. Take a tiny ball of paste and gently thin out one edge with your thumb to create a petal shape. Completely wrap this around the cone to form the bud, nipping in the paste at the middle to form a waist.

2 Make another two petals in the same way and wrap them around, overlapping each other at the middle. and gently nipping in again. This is a small rose or bud.

3 For a full rose, add another three petals and overlap them. You can add as many more petals as you wish. Gently pull or bend the edges of the petals outwards to create the required realistic rose effect.

4 Check that the waist of the flower is tightly pinched and cut off the excess. Leave the finished roses on greaseproof paper in a cool dry place to dry overnight.

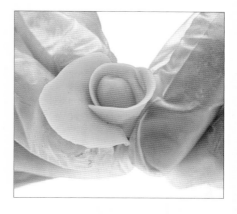

Coating Marzipan Shapes
Marzipan shapes can be dipped in melted chocolate. They can be sprayed with colour diluted with alcohol, with confectioner's varnish, gum arabic solution or melted cocoa butter to give a good glaze.

Marzipan Tips
- Thin plastic or rubber gloves prevent strong colours from staining your hands. You can shape petals or other fine shapes more easily wearing them than working between sheets of cellophane or cling film.
- Keep marzipan wrapped tightly when not in use.
- Use natural marzipan for a better colour.
- For long storage, paint the modelled item with confectioner's glaze.
- Read the manufacturer's instructions carefully when buying food glaze or varnishes.

Marzipan Flowers

Flowers that can be made in sugar paste or pastillage can also be made using marzipan. A little sugar paste or pastillage should be added to strengthen the marzipan. Use coloured marzipan or paint the finished flowers. They may also be sugar glazed by dipping in syrup boiled to 150°C/300°F, the 'hard crack' stage. This should be done after the flowers have been dried out for at least 24 hours. Flowers to be dipped in syrup must be made a little thicker. Pierce a wire rod or fork into the base for dipping and place on an oiled tray to set.

Simple flowers can be quickly cut out with small cutters. Using coloured marzipan – pale pink, yellow or purple – cut with a small blossom cutter and place on sponge to dry. Cut a bought stamen with a round head to the length required and dip the head in edible glue. Push it through the centre of the flower until secured and leave to set.

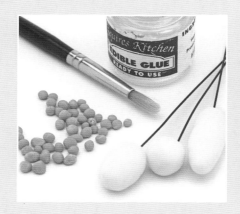  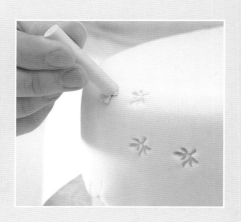

 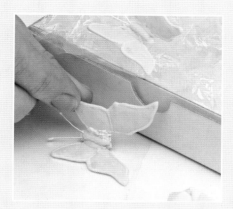 

Cakes for All Occasions

This brilliant collection of decorated cakes has everything to offer – good looks, irresistible flavours and contemporary styles. There are designs for every season and celebration, including favourite recipes and classic finishes, as well as cakes with a distinctly modern appeal.

Decorating a cake is enjoyable and producing a party piece need not be daunting. This inspiring chapter will help you to create stunning centrepieces with confidence. Whether you are catering for a birthday, anniversary, formal occasion or fun gathering you will find just the right idea. Discover that making a stunning wedding cake is perfectly possible using a deceptively simple yet stylish design.

You can make a cake for the sheer fun of being creative and sharing something special. There is no need to wait for an annual event before trying many of these recipes – whip up an indulgent chocolate creation; bake a pyramid of fairy cakes; go retro with little fancies; or zest up the day with a glorious citrus gâteau.

Iced Fairy Cakes

The great thing about making lots of little cakes is you can vary the toppings to suit your guests, your children or your mood and have fun with several different ideas at the same time.

Makes about 15

1 x 3-egg quantity Victoria Sponge
    mixture (page 16)

1-2tsp cocoa powder

2-3tsp milk

5 cherries with stalks

2 quantities Glacé Icing (page 24)

2tbsp Chocolate Butter Icing (page 23)

5 chocolate shapes (page 43)

icing sugar, sifted

red or blue edible food colouring

silver dragees

coloured stars

1 Preheat the oven to 180°C/350°F/gas mark 4. Prepare the sponge mixture. Prepare 15 paper cake cases in a patty tin. Mix the cocoa powder with the milk and use to flavour about one third of the mixture. Spoon the mixtures into the cake cases and bake for 15-20 minutes until evenly risen, lightly browned and just firm to the touch. Transfer to a wire rack and leave until cold.

2 Set aside five plain cakes, selecting those that are more domed. Colour 1tbsp of the glacé icing red or blue. Spoon white glacé icing over the remaining plain fairy cakes. Add drops of coloured icing and then swirl the coloured icing into the white with a cocktail stick. Finish with silver dragees or coloured stars.

3 Place a cherry on each of the reserved plain cakes, keeping them in place with a little glacé icing. Holding the cherry stalk to keep the fruit in place, pour about 1tbsp glacé icing over the cherry. Add extra icing if necessary, to coat the cake. Leave to set firm.

4 Cut a small lid off the top of each chocolate cake. Pipe a swirl of butter icing into the centre of each. Replace the lid on top. Add a chocolate shape and sift a little icing sugar over the top.

Frosted Fruits Gâteau

Most fruits take sugar frosting but the smaller fruit on stalks look the best. Autumn berries are good if they are still firm. Any very soft or slightly blemished fruit will not work well as they do not dry out fully. When well coated with sugar fruit will keep for several days in a dry atmosphere.

Serves 6-8

175g (6oz) mixed firm berries

110g (4oz) mixed fruits, such as cherries, redcurrants and physallis

1 small egg white

75g (3oz) caster sugar

18cm (7in) Genoese Sponge (page 17)

300ml (1/2pint) double cream

1 Set aside the softer and larger berries for the filling, cutting them in half if necessary. Dry the fruit thoroughly on paper towel.

2 Put the egg white in a small bowl and beat very slightly to loosen it. Put the sugar in a larger bowl. Cover a clean tray with greaseproof paper.

3 Brush the fruit thinly but evenly with egg white, brushing into the cracks and crevices.

4 Then coat thoroughly in the sugar by dipping the fruit and sprinkling with sugar. Place on the greaseproof paper. Leave in a warm dry place for several hours or until the sugar coating is completely dry and crisp.

5 Whip the cream until it stands in soft peaks. Sandwich the sponge layers with about a third of the cream and the reserved berries. Spread a little cream over the top and pipe the rest around the top edge of the sponge.

6 Place the sponge on a serving plate. Arrange the frosted fruits on top of the cake.

Frosting Tips

• Fruit for frosting should be clean and dry.

• Repeat the coating process for the best result.

• For longer keeping, store the fruit in an airtight container. Add a little salt or silica crystals wrapped in a twist of fine fabric to absorb any moisture.

Carrot Cake

This moist and more-ish cake is covered in a rich and naughty topping. The decorative marzipan carrots and cinnamon sticks are fun to make, especially as they can be prepared well ahead and stored in an airtight tin.

Serves 16

175ml (5fl oz) sunflower oil
175g (6oz) soft light brown sugar
3 large eggs, beaten
finely grated zest of 1 orange and juice
    of 1/2 orange
275g (10oz) self-raising wholemeal flour
1tsp baking powder
110g (4oz) sultanas
450g (1lb) carrots, peeled and finely
    grated

Topping and decoration
1 quantity American Frosting (page 25)
100g (3½oz) Marzipan (page 26)
brown and terracotta edible food
    colourings
angelica or glacé lime peel

1 Make the decorations first. Colour two-thirds of the marzipan terracotta and use to make carrots (see page 44). Use a cocktail stick to mark the characteristic indents and brush a little colouring into the cracks. Push tiny sticks of angelica or glacé lime peel into the tops for stalks.

2 Colour the rest of the marzipan brown and roll out thinly. Roll tiny pieces into sticks to resemble cinnamon sticks, then cut or fray the edges. Leave to dry out.

3 Preheat the oven to 180°C/350°F/gas mark 4. Line and grease a 23cm (9in) round tin. Blend all the cake ingredients in a bowl and beat thoroughly. Spoon the mixture into the prepared tin and smooth it evenly.

4 Bake for 40-50 minutes, until the cake is risen and firm to the touch. Leave to cool in the tin then transfer to a wire rack.

5 Prepare the American frosting. Spread the frosting all over the cake, peaking and swirling it attractively. Place on a serving dish. Arrange the carrots and cinnamon sticks on the cake shortly before serving.

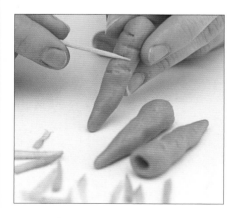
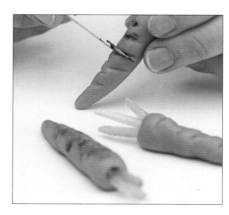

Serves 8-10

250g (9oz) dark chocolate
175g (6oz) unsalted butter
6 eggs, separated
200g (7oz) caster sugar
50g (2oz) self-raising flour
3-4tbsp rum

Icing and Decoration
1 quantity dark chocolate Ganache
   (page 41)
75g (3oz) white chocolate
110g (4oz) dark chocolate

Tipsy Chocolate Treat

This indulgent, grown-up dark chocolate cake is well laced with rum underneath the drizzled chocolate decoration.

1 Line and grease a deep 20cm (8in) round loose-bottomed tin. Preheat the oven to 170°C/325°F/gas mark 3. Melt the chocolate and butter gently in a heatproof bowl over a saucepan of hot water. Alternatively, melt in the microwave for 30–50 seconds at a time on medium. Leave to cool slightly.

2 Whisk the egg yolks with 150g (5oz) of the sugar until pale, thick and creamy. Gently stir in the cooled chocolate. Then fold in the flour.

3 In a separate bowl, whisk the egg whites until stiff but not dry. Then gently whisk in the rest of the sugar. Fold the whites into the chocolate mixture and spoon the mixture into the prepared tin.

4 Bake for 1 hour 15 minutes, until the cake is well risen and springy to the touch. A knife should come out clean and free of sticky mixture. Leave to part-cool in the tin, then turn out onto a wire rack and leave until cold.

5 Invert the sponge and sprinkle the rum over its base. Allow to soak in for a few minutes. Then turn the cake the right way up on the rack. Stand the rack over a tray or paper. Reserve a third of the ganache. Quickly pour the rest all over the cake. Make sure all the cake is covered and save the drips of excess ganache that have fallen onto the tray or paper.

7 Cut a piece of foil and mark a rectangle about 25cm x 7.5cm (10in x 3in) on it. Have a rolling pin ready. Melt the white and dark chocolate separately and spoon into small paper piping bags. Snip off the points for piping finely. Drizzle white chocolate in lines across the top of the cake.

8 Drizzle the dark chocolate on the foil first, then the white chocolate, keeping within the marked rectangle. Reserve the unused chocolate. Carefully drape the foil over the rolling pin and leave to set. When firm, carefully remove pieces of the drizzled chocolate semi-circles and arrange several on top of the cake.

9 Transfer the cake to a serving plate. Re-melt the remaining ganache and chocolate together and allow to cool until thick enough to pipe. Then pipe around the base of the cake. Keep in a cool place until ready to serve.

Retro Iced Fancies

Originally called *fondant fancies* and covered with a soft fondant icing, these favourites of a bygone era seem to have taken on a new lease of life. Here they are coated with soft royal icing instead of the traditional fondant. Glacé icing will not do. They can be made in whatever shape and colour you like, but look particularly attractive in soft pastel shades.

Makes 10-12

2-egg Victoria Sponge baked in a
    15cm (6in) square or a rectangular
    tin (page 16)
1/2 quantity Royal Icing made with
    225g (8oz) icing sugar (page 28)
edible food colouring
few blanched almonds or pieces of
    candied peel

1 Cut the cake into bite-size squares, circles, triangles or other shapes, such as crescents and diamonds. Place on a wire rack.

2 Divide the icing among three bowls. Keep one portion white and cover it closely with cling film. Colour the other two portions as you wish, then gently dilute them with a little water or lemon juice to a pouring consistency – just a little thicker than for run-outs.

3 Coat half the batch of cakes with one colour and half with the other. If the coats are thin, repeat once the first coat has dried. Place a piece of peel or an almond on some of the cakes before you coat them.

4 Colour the reserved white icing two or more different colours and use to pipe or drizzle designs on the cakes. Leave one colour to set fully before adding another colour. Leave to set before serving.

Icing Tip
Fondant icing can be bought in the form of packet mix from specialist cake decorating suppliers. It can be made up as directed and used for these iced fancies for a truly authentic effect.

Orange and Lemon Gâteau

What can you do with a frozen sponge cake? Simple, slice the layers and sandwich them together with tangy lemon curd. Coat in a fruity butter icing and top with candied shreds of orange rind and shards of caramelised sugar. Nothing to it really!

Serves 10–12

5 or 6 thin layers lemon Victoria Sponge (page 16) or Madeira Cake (page 18)

2 quantities lemon Butter Icing (page 23) or Meringue Butter Icing (page 24)

1 large orange

40g (1¹/₂oz) caster sugar

2tbsp orange juice

6tbsp lemon curd

25g (1oz) granulated sugar

25cm (10in) round gold cake board

1 Chill the thin cake layers. Prepare the butter icing and leave to firm up.

2 Use a vegetable peeler to cut thin strips of orange rind, avoiding the white pith or trimming it off. Then cut into fine strips. Dissolve the caster sugar in the orange juice in a small saucepan. Add the strips of rind and simmer gently until the sugar has almost caramelised and all the liquid has evaporated.

3 Tip the rinds onto a sheet of non-stick baking paper. Separate the strands and leave in an airy room that is not too cool or damp until hardened.

4 Sandwich the sponge layers together alternately with lemon curd and a third of the butter icing. Lightly cover the top and sides with butter icing, finishing with a simple swirled or knife-mark pattern. Chill until ready to serve.

5 Meanwhile, sprinkle the granulated sugar on a small sheet of foil. Place under a hot grill until the sugar has dissolved and is bubbling and golden brown. Set aside to cool.

6 Place the cake on the board. Just before serving arrange the shreds of orange rind in a pile in the centre of the cake. Break the caramel into shards or large pieces. Arrange some caramel pieces with the orange rind on top and some around the edge of the cake.

Battenberg Cake

This unique cake is ideal for lovers of marzipan. It was apparently named after the marriage of Queen Victoria's granddaughter to Prince Louis of Battenberg in 1884. Our recipe has a choice of three flavour combinations.

Serves 6-8

1 x 4-egg Victoria Sponge mixture
(page 16) flavoured and coloured with
vanilla; orange and chocolate; or
lemon and orange
2-3tbsp apricot jam
300g (10oz) Marzipan (page 26), flavoured
with 3tbsp sifted cocoa powder for the
chocolate cake
caster sugar
pink and green edible food colouring if
making the vanilla cake

1 Preheat the oven to 180°C/350°F/gas mark 4. Line and grease a 18cm (7in) shallow square baking tin. Cut a strip of double greaseproof paper and grease it. Use this to divide the tin in half.

2 Prepare the sponge mixture, flavour it with vanilla, if liked, and divide in half. Colour the vanilla portions pink and green. Alternatively, instead of vanilla, use chocolate in one portion and orange in the other; or lemon in one portion and orange in the other. Colour the orange portion with a little orange food colouring.

3 Spoon one mixture into half the prepared baking tin, keeping the paper in the middle, and the rest in the other side. Try to make the divide as straight as possible. Bake in the middle of the oven for 35-40 minutes. Turn out and cool on a wire rack.

4 When cool, trim the edges and cut the cake portions lengthways in half, making four equal parts. Warm the jam in a small saucepan. Brush two sides of each portion of cake with jam and stick them together to give a chequerboard effect.

5 Roll out the marzipan to a rectangle wide and long enough to wrap around the cake. Trim the edges neatly. Brush the outside of the cake with jam. Place the cake on the marzipan and wrap the paste around the cake. Dampen the edges lightly to form a neat join at one of the corners of the cake.

6 Pinch the top and bottom edges of the paste into a pattern with crimpers. Use the extra marzipan to make marzipan flowers and leaves in various colours or other decorations of your choice.

Sunburst

Something to celebrate – a christening or a new house perhaps? Whatever the reason, bring some added sunshine to the occasion with this quick and simple, three-dimensional design with sparkle and silver shimmer.

Serves: 16-20

20cm (8in) square Golden Fruit Cake
   (page 21)

2tbsp Apricot Glaze (page 26)

225g (8oz) Marzipan (optional, page 26)

550g (1¹/₂lb) Sugar Paste (page 30)

yellow and blue edible food colours

blue sequin ribbon

yellow sparkles

silver moon dust

turquoise balls

25cm (10in) square cake board

1 Brush the cake with apricot glaze, then cover with the marzipan, if using, or cover with sugar paste alone. Use about two-thirds of the sugar paste to cover the cake, reserving the rest for decoration. Transfer the cake to the board.

2 Colour two-thirds of the remaining sugar paste pale turquoise (using blue and yellow) and one-third pale yellow. Wrap in cling film. Roll out a quarter of the turquoise paste and use to cover the board. Then frill the edge with a cocktail stick or frilling tool (page 40). Trim the base of the cake and the board with sequin ribbon.

3 Roll out the yellow paste quite thickly and cut a 4-5cm (1¹/₂-2in) circle for the sun. Cut out 7-8 strips shaped from narrow to wide for the sun's rays. Attach the sun and the rays to the top of the cake with a little water.

4 Roll out the rest of the turquoise paste quite thickly and cut out a variety of cloud-like shapes. Use the blunt ends of different-sized round cutters and the wide ends of piping nozzles to make the shapes and cut a third of the circle. Use a fine, sharp, pointed knife to cut out the marked shapes of larger clouds. Cut away some of the centres to increase the curve. Layer the clouds over the sun's rays, raising some pieces for a three dimensional effect. Cut several tiny raindrops from the remaining blue paste.

5 Sprinkle the sun with yellow sparkles. Using a damp brush, brush the clouds with moon dust. Finally, place the turquoise balls on the board at the base of the cake with a little icing.

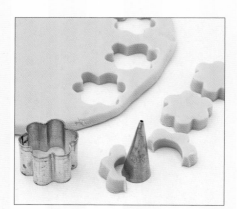

Chocolate Heaven

A glamorous casing of chocolate ganache and a topping of tiny alcoholic truffles transform a simple chocolate sponge into a stunning dinner party gâteau or centrepiece for almost any occasion.

Serves 8-12

300ml (¹/₂ pint) double cream
2-4tbsp brandy, whisky or Courvoisier
18cm (7in) chocolate Genoese Sponge
    (page 17)
1 quantity Ganache (page 41)
25g (1oz) icing sugar, sifted
25g (1oz) cocoa powder, sifted
Chocolate Leaves (page 42)

1 Whip the cream lightly. Take a third of the cream and stir in half the brandy, whisky or Courvoisier. Sandwich the sponge layers together with this and place on a serving plate.

2 Cut a strip of foil at least the length of the cake circumference and twice the height of the side. Spread one third of the warm ganache over this, making the base edge straight along the foil, but the top edge attractively jagged. Leave to set but do not allow to become hard.

3 Divide the remaining ganache in half. Beat half the remaining cream into one portion of ganache and continue to beat lightly until it thickens to a spreading consistency. Swirl this over the top of the cake and spread it around the sides.

4 For the truffles, mix the remaining ganache with the remaining alcohol and cream and the icing sugar. Beat well, then place in the refrigerator to set.

5 Wrap the just-set chocolate case around the cake, jagged edge up, and gently peel off the foil as you press the chocolate onto the cake. Press the edges to seal. Chill the cake until the chocolate is firm.

6 Dust your hands with cocoa and roll small teaspoons of the truffle mixture into tiny balls. Chill again. When ready to serve, carefully arrange the truffles on the top of the cake, adding some on the serving plate. Dust with more cocoa powder and finish with a few chocolate leaves.

Berrytime

Realistic-looking three-dimensional raspberries, blackberries and tayberries can all be made by hand with a little time and patience then individual berries can be wired together with leaves. Flat, or bas relief, berries, to fit on the vertical sides of a cake, can be made in flexible plastic moulds. Moulds are also available for making detailed clusters of berries and leaves. A combination of moulds and cutters works well.

Serves 10-12

20cm (8in) round Golden Fruit Cake
   (page 21)
450g (1lb) Marzipan (page 26)
675g (1½lb) Sugar Paste (page 30)
Raspberry pink, blackberry and leaf
   green gel or dust colours
225g (8oz) bought flower paste mix
floristry wire (24-26 gauge)
green and brown floristry tape (known as
   gutta percha)
edible glue
25cm (10in) square cake board

1 Cover the cake with marzipan. Colour three quarters of the sugar paste a shade of raspberry pink and use to cover the cake. Cover the board with white sugar paste and top with sugar paste that you have coloured grass green.

2 Make up the flower paste according to the packet instructions. Knead until thoroughly workable. Use about a quarter to fill individual berry moulds lightly dusted with cornflour, if using. Turn out and leave to harden in a warm dry place for at least 24 hours. Paint the shapes the colours of the berries and leaves using diluted gel or dry powders.

3 Colour about a quarter of the remaining flower paste a shade of raspberry pink. Mould about 15 pea-sized round or pear-shaped white balls for cores and attach them to 15cm (6in) lengths floristry wire. To do this, make a tiny hook at one end of the wire to hold paste and moisten the wire with glue. Leave to dry for 1-2 hours.

4 For each berry roll 20-30 tiny balls of pink paste and attach them to the cores with glue. Shape gently with your fingers and leave to dry for 1-2 hours. Support the wires in a block of floristry foam while the paste is drying.

5 For the calyx (the leafy cup which holds the berry), colour the rest of the paste leaf green. Roll out a small piece of paste thinly and cut out a small calyx. Gently flatten out the points with a dog-bone tool. Place the paste on a piece of foam and then push in the centre to give it a cup shape. Push a berry wire through the centre, brush the paste with glue and secure the calyx to the berry. Bend the points with a paintbrush to give a life-like shape.

6 Cut out several leaves from the green sugar paste. Vein them with a vein marker and shape them gently, then attach to wires with glue. Leave everything to set hard under a lamp for 24 hours.

7 Tint the berries and leaves with shades of purple and green-brown, respectively. Take 2-3 berries and 2-3 leaves, and wrap their wires together with green tape to make a small bunch.

8 Arrange the bunches and the moulded fruits on and around the cake, attaching them with edible glue.

Petal Power Cake

This charming flower-covered creation is perfect for Mother's day instead of a bunch of flowers. Use freesias instead of roses, if you like, and colour the cake to match the colours of the petals.

Serves 6-8

20cm (8in) Madeira or Golden Fruit Cake
    (pages 18 or 21)
2tbsp Apricot Glaze (page 26)
350g (12oz) Marzipan (page 26)
450g (1lb) Sugar Paste (page 30)
3-4 roses in full bloom
1 small egg white, lightly beaten
25g (1oz) caster sugar
edible food colours to match roses
edible leaf green dusting powder
25cm (10in) round cake board

1 Using the template on page 96, cut the cake into a petal shape. Brush with apricot glaze and cover with marzipan. Set aside for several hours. Cover the board with coloured paper to match the flowers if you wish.

2 Discard any blemished petals and put the best ones on a board covered with greaseproof paper. Save the buds or centres of the roses to decorate the board.

3 Brush the petals thinly with egg white. Then sprinkle them with sugar to coat them evenly and fairly thickly. Leave on the paper for several hours to dry and harden.

4 Colour the remaining sugar paste to match the petals, marbling the colours if you wish. Remove about a fifth of the paste, then cover the cake with the rest. Place the cake on the board.

5 Using a sugar paste gun and the reserved coloured or white sugar paste, make sufficient rope to wrap around the edge of the cake. The white paste can be coloured first, if liked. Twist two lengths of different-coloured ropes together for an attractive effect.

6 Use a tiny flower embosser to mark a delicate pattern all over the cake. Brush a little dusting powder in a pale leaf green into these indents (page 40).

7 Arrange a selection of sugared petals on top of the cake and on the board. Add the reserved flower buds for a finishing touch.

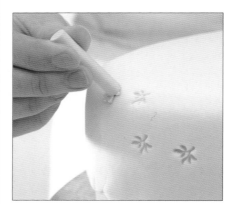

Storing sugared roses
Sugared rose petals will keep well in an airtight container for a couple of weeks. To help keep them dry, add a little salt or silica crystals tied up in a small piece of muslin to absorb moisture.

Butterfly Thank You Cake

Individual cakes make the perfect gift, particularly as a Thank You. Why not make one large square cake and cut it into four? Freeze the remaining sections so you always have a small cake ready to be transformed into an impromptu gift.

Serves 2-4

10cm (4in) square Dark Rich Fruit Cake
    or Madeira Cake (pages 20 or 18)
1tbsp Apricot Glaze (page 26)
175g (6oz) Marzipan (page 26)
1/2 quantity Royal Icing (page 28) plus
    1 quantity Royal Icing without glycerine
pink and hyacinth edible food colour
    powders
white stamens and coloured stamens
2-3 prepared leaves

1 Brush the cake with apricot glaze and cover with marzipan. Leave to dry for 24 hours. Over the next couple of days give the cake one coat of white and two coats of lavender royal icing. Leave to dry thoroughly.

2 Meanwhile, make up the royal icing without glycerine. Colour half pink and half a light lavender colour. Use pink and hyacinth colours to achieve the right shades. Using the template on page 96 and run-out instructions on page 37, make 6-8 of the small flat run-out butterflies in lavender with pink dots. Leave to in a cool place to harden.

3 Make 3-4 medium-sized pink butterfly run-out pieces with lavender dots. Attach white stamens to the body while still wet. Leave to dry. Pipe a tiny amount of pink icing on either side of the body pieces and attach the wings. Raise the wings slightly and support them on a soft curved surface so they dry raised.

4 Use some of the remaining lavender icing to pipe tiny dots and lines around the top edge of the cake. Attach a small bunch of coloured stamens and two leaves to the top of the cake. Position one butterfly on the bunch of stamens. Add as many more butterflies as you wish, attaching smaller ones around the sides. Butterflies can be attached to a gift box for the cake.

5 Support the cake on folds of matching tissue paper and place in a small cake box.

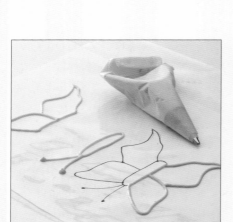

Spring is Here

This light, fresh design suits Easter or any spring event. If you like the classic simnel cake, use the dark fruit cake recipe and place a layer of marzipan in the middle of the mixture as you fill the tin before baking.

1 Brush the cake with apricot glaze and cover with marzipan. Coat the cake and the board with royal icing and leave to dry. Reserve 1-2 tbsp royal icing if possible, for attaching the flowers.

2 Make up the flower paste or pastillage as directed on the packet. Colour one third of the paste yellow and one third pale green. Use blossom cutters to to cut out 12 large blossoms and 12 small blossoms out of the white paste. Cut 12 small blossoms from the yellow paste. Shape the petals with a frilling tool.

3 Pipe white centres in the yellow blossoms with royal icing. Colour a little royal icing pale yellow and pipe yellow centres in the white blossoms.

4 Use the green paste to make 26-30 leaves. Press between leaf veiners to shape and thin out. Curve the leaves slightly to give a natural effect. Set aside to dry.

5 Attach the small flowers, with leaves, around the base of the cake. Position an arrangement of the larger flowers, with leaves, on the top of the cake.

6 Tie a double yellow ribbon around the cake and add any remaining flowers or leaves around the base.

Serves 16-20

20cm (8in) round Golden Fruit Cake
    (page 21)
3tbsp Apricot Glaze (page 26)
450g (1lb) Marzipan (page 26)
1 quantity Royal Icing (page 28)
175g (6oz) bought flower paste
    or pastillage mix
saffron yellow and leaf-green edible
    food colours
yellow ribbon
25cm (10in) round cake board

Birthday Bonanza

For some Birthday celebrations you just want to go a little crazy and this cake suits that mood perfectly. Whatever the age, candles, sparklers, streamers and party poppers create the required sparkle and party impression.

Serves 16-18

110g (4oz) bought pastillage mix

orange, sunflower and terracotta edible
   paste colours

gold wires

edible glue

bronze or gold dusting powder

4-6 tiny polystyrene balls

23cm (9in) round Madeira Cake (page 18)

110g (4oz) lemon-flavoured Butter Icing
   (page 23)

550g (1¼lb) Sugar Paste (page 30)

party poppers, sparklers, long sparkly
   party candles, fine gold ribbon,

28cm (11in) thin board covered with
   bronze wrapping paper

1 Make up the pastillage as directed on the packet and colour it a strong sunflower yellow. Marble half the paste with orange and terracotta streaks. Wrap the rest tightly in cling film and set aside.

2 Roll the marbled pastillage out thinly. Cut into about 20 long thin triangles to resemble flames for the central pieces of the explosion. Attach half to gold wires with glue and leave to set. Lay the rest over a rolling pin so they dry in a curved shape.

3 Attach polystyrene balls to wires with glue. Dust your hands with cornflour, flatten hazelnut-sized pieces of yellow or marbled pastillage in the palm of your hands until thin enough to wrap around the wetted polystyrene balls (as for marzipan roses page 45). Shape these into balloons and leave to harden. Paint or dust with gold if you wish. Leave all decorations to dry for at least a day.

4 Reserve 1-2tbsp of the butter icing and use the rest to coat the cake. Mix any excess pastillage with a little sugar paste, flatten it to a thick domed round about 5cm (2in) across and centre it on top of the cake.

5 Colour the sugar paste a rich burnt orange. Roll out to about 40cm (16in) and lay carefully over the cake, making sure it is centred. From the centre cut triangles over the dome and pull them out for explosive effect. Support these pieces on crumpled soft paper or cotton wool. Flatten the paste on the sides of the cake and trim. Gently brush the cake all over with bronze powder. Leave to set for about a day.

6 Attach the curved marbled orange flames to the centre with butter icing. Push the wires of the remaining flames and balloons gently into the centre of the cake. Add candles, sparklers, gold ribbons, party poppers and streamers to create a party centrepiece. Light all the candles and sparklers just before serving.

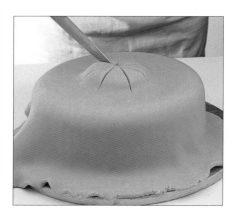

Birthday Surprises

These little boxes can be made in any mix of colours – all white and pearly would be very sophisticated for a 21st birthday or for a wedding cake for instance, or try a mix of candy colours for a little girl or boy's birthday. Work out your cake tin and box sizes before you start, allowing for the two larger sizes to be made up of two layers of sponge.

Serves 16-20

10-egg Madeira Cake mix (page 18)
    baked in either a 28cm (11in) square
    or 20cm x 25cm (8in x 10in)
    rectangular tin
2 quantities Butter Icing (page 23)
1kg (2¼lb) Sugar Paste (page 30)
bluebell blue edible food colouring
white and blue sugar-coated chocolate
    sweets such as Smarties
20cm (8in) square cake board

1 Thoroughly chill the cake. Cut out cubes of about the following sizes: 11cm (4½ in), 8.5cm (3½ in), 6cm (2½in) and 2.5cm (1in). The two larger cubes may have to be made from two stacked layers of sponge sandwiched together with butter icing. Make as many of the small ones as you like to add around the base.

2 To create the tumbling effect, cut a corner wedge off the second and third boxes, making sure they stand securely on the cut corners. Wrap the sponges individually in cling film until required.

3 Colour half the sugar past blue, wrap in cling film and set aside. Roll out half the white sugar paste and cut four 11cm (4½in) squares. Spread the cake sides with butter icing and carefully attach the paste sides one at a time, sealing the corners neatly.

4 Measure the remaining two sides before you cut the paste, as they will now be slightly larger than first sides. Attach the paste in the same way.

5 Cover the remaining boxes, taking care at all the corners to keep them in a good sharp shape. Cover the board with the remaining sugar paste.

6 Stack all the boxes, attaching them with a little butter icing and set aside to firm up for a few hours. At the last minute, just before serving the cake, attach the sugar sweets with butter icing.

21st Birthday

Everyone loves a fairy cake and this impressive collection suits any age, and almost any occasion. A good strong colour theme is important; matched with lots of ideas for the individual toppings and you have a fun recipe for success. Make plenty of cakes, as they are sure to go!

Makes about 30

1 quantity Carrot Cake mixture (page 52)
silver cup cake cases
450g (1lb) Royal Icing (page 28)
blue edible food colouring
50g (2oz) Sugar Paste (page 30)
silver candles, balls, ribbons and/or
    netting to decorate
edible blue or sliver glitter
blue and silver ribbon
two- or three-tier cake stand

1 Preheat the oven to 180°C/350°F/gas mark 4. Place 30 silver cake cases in patty tins. Make the carrot cake mixture and divide it among the cake cases. Bake for about 20 minutes, until evenly risen, lightly browned and springy to touch. Allow to cool on wire racks.

2 Colour half the icing pale blue. Ice half the cakes with white icing and half with blue. Top some of the cakes with silver balls, arranged in '21' shapes, while the icing is wet. Leave to set for several hours or overnight.

3 Colour or marble the sugar paste with blue. Roll out half thinly and cut out star or flower shapes. Roll the rest of the paste into ropes and shape into the numerals one and two, small enough to fit on the cakes. Leave these decorations to dry.

4 Colour some of the royal icing a darker shade of blue. Choose a variety of piped designs, such as dots, lattice, diagonal lines, circles and flowers, and decorate five or more cakes in similar designs, using different colourways. Simple designs using contrasting colours are very effective. Add numbers, stars, candles, streamers and/or glitter, to some of the cakes. Use a limited number of different designs and make several cakes of each type. Leave to set.

5 To serve, arrange all the cakes in a pile on a two- or three-tiered cake stand. Make sure cakes with candles are stable and upright. Tie a big ribbon around the base of the stand and light the candles.

Cup cake tip
Bite-size cup cakes are stylish and fun. Make them in petit four cases, reducing the cooking time to 10-15 minutes. Keep all the decorations miniature in proportion with the tiny cakes.

Valentine's Cake

Fine candy-coloured stripes are easy and effective. A few silver balls and a centrepiece of sugar paste hearts finish this stylish design for a striking result.

Serves 6-8

1 quantity Madeira Cake (page 18) baked
    in an 18-20cm (7-8in) heart-shaped tin
3tbsp Apricot Glaze (page 26) or
    Butter Icing (page 23)
375g (12oz) Marzipan (page 26)
450g (1lb) Sugar Paste (page 30)
edible glue
silver balls
pink ribbon
23cm (11in) heart-shaped cake board

1 Brush the cake with apricot glaze and cover with marzipan. Leave to dry for 12-24 hours. Colour two-thirds of the sugar paste a very pale pink and cover the cake with this. Keep any leftover sugar paste in a small polythene bag.

2 Measure the cake diagonally across the middle and down both sides. Colour the rest of the sugar paste candy pink and roll it out to a thick strip about 7-8cm (3in) wide and the length measured. Cut into several thin strips.

3 Starting at the middle of the cake, which will require the longest strip, use a ruler to paint a straight line of glue across the top of the cake and down the sides. Place the strip of paste in position. Press gently into place. Lay the remaining strips across the cake in the same way. Keep the strips 2.5cm (1in) apart. Measure the positions precisely for straight, even lines. Cut the strips off neatly at the base. Save any excess sugar paste.

4 Place the cake on a heart-shaped board covered with white tissue paper or white sugar paste. Roll out the remaining sugar paste thickly and cut-out heart shapes in various sizes. Attach tiny hearts around the base of the board and slightly larger hearts on the cake.

5 Cut out a few large hearts. Cut out some hollow middles by using a smaller heart-shaped cutter. Attach small heart shapes to some of the larger shapes. Leave the shapes to harden – they are to stand up in the centre of the cake. The large hearts should be supported on soft icing or attached to the cake with glue. Finally, add silver balls around the base of the cake and trim the board with pink ribbon.

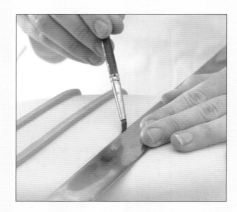

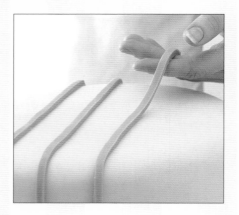

Engagement Ring Cake

This ring theme is one that you can also adapt for weddings and anniversaries. Try covering the cake with edible gold for a very special celebration.

Serves 16-20

100g (3¹/₂oz) bought petal paste or
    pastillage mix
blue edible food colouring
6-8tbsp Royal Icing (page 28)
silver or pearl balls
silver snowflake dusting powder
3-egg Madeira Cake mixture (page 18)
50g (2oz) Butter Icing (page 23)
1kg (2¹/₄lb) Sugar Paste (page 30)
28cm (11in) square cake board
fresh flowers

1 Before starting the cake, make up the petal paste or pastillage. Make a selection of blossoms and flowers in white and blue. Cut out the flower and blossom shapes and press them between rubber moulds lightly dusted with cornflour. With a spot of icing, fix pearl or silver balls in the flower centres. Make a selection of rose leaves and dust them with silver snowflake dust. Leave to dry.

2 Preheat the oven to180°C/350°F/gas mark 4. Grease and flour a 23cm (9in) savarin tin or ring mould. Fill with the cake mixture, rounding the top, and bake for 40-50 minutes, until a skewer comes out free of sticky mixture. Leave in the tin to cool.

3 Remove the cake from the tin and freeze for 1-2 hours before covering. Coat the board with royal icing. When the cake is part-frozen, trim off the flat edge around the top rim and round it into a smooth and evenly-domed shape.

4 Coat the cake with butter icing. Roll out the sugar paste into a circle 5-7.5cm (2-3in) larger than the ring. Allow plenty of paste to cover the underneath of the cake. Lift the paste carefully using a rolling pin and place it carefully over the ring, letting as much as possible fall into the hole in the centre. Smooth the paste over the top and sides.

5 Turn the cake over. Make one slit in the centre of the excess paste and carefully pull the pieces through to cover the inside rim. Gently work the paste up to cover the rest of the cake and smooth out any joins.

6 Turn the cake back over, correct way up and, with your hands or smoothers, ease out any creases in the paste. Dust all over with snowflake dust. Place on the board.

7 Use a little royal icing to attach the large flowers to the cake and smaller flowers around them. Arrange the remaining paste flowers on the board together with some fresh flowers.

Checkmate

Lashings of chocolate and a tempting challenge especially for the man in your life! If you want to make a real game, buy a full set of chocolate chessmen... but this does mean that the cake cannot be eaten until the game is over.

Serves 18-20

450g (1lb) Sugar Paste (page 30) blended with 50g (2oz) melted dark or white chocolate (see step 1) or
450g (1lb) chocolate modelling paste
Double quantity of Madeira Cake mixture (page 18), flavoured with 1tbsp instant coffee dissolved in 2tsp boiling water, baked in a 23cm (9in) square cake tin
1/2 quantity Butter Icing (page 23) flavoured with coffee or chocolate
75g (3oz) each white and dark chocolate
1/2 quantity each of white and dark chocolate Ganache (page 41), cooled to a piping consistency
gold rope
thin brown ribbon
28cm (11in) square gold board

1 Work the sugar paste until soft and smooth. Then gradually work in the cooled melted chocolate, kneading it on a clean work surface until thoroughly blended. Add sifted icing sugar if necessary.

2 Coat the cake with butter icing. Roll out a third of the chocolate paste to a square the size of the top of the cake and lay it on neatly. Roll out four pieces to fit the sides. Attach them and then gently mould the corners together. Smooth over the sides and top to get neat square corners.

3 Place the cake on the gold board. Trim the base and top edges with twisted gold rope and brown ribbon. Leave until firm.

4 Melt the white and dark chocolates separately and spread out smoothly and evenly on sheets of foil. Leave to cool. Before the chocolate sets too hard, cut out small squares, making at least 20 of each type to allow for breakages.

5 Make the ganache and allow to cool to piping consistency. On greaseproof paper or non-stick backing parchment, pipe 10-12 or more rosettes in each colour, making them as tall or pointed as you can. Make the white a different shape from the dark shapes if you wish. Leave the shapes to set firmly in the refrigerator.

6 Attach the chocolate squares to the top of the cake, using any remaining butter icing or melted chocolate to keep them in place. Add the chocolate rosettes.

Winter Blues

This jolly scene makes a delightful Christmas cake with plenty of fun modelling and challenging finger work for young cooks. The penguins are, in fact, quite simple to make but you may end up with black fingers!

Serves 10-12

1 quantity Dark Rich Fruit Cake mixture
(page 20) baked in an oval cake tin
20cm x 14cm (8in x 6in)
Apricot Glaze (page 26)
450g (1lb) Marzipan (page 26)
1 quantity Royal Icing (page 28)
bluebell blue and orange berberis edible
food colour
110g (4oz) Sugar Paste (page 30)
110g (4oz) bought black sugar paste
daffodil dusting powder
clear snowflake sparkles
edible glue
25cm (10in) silver oval cake board

1 Brush the cake with apricot glaze and cover with marzipan. Coat the top with white royal icing. Colour the rest pale blue and ice the side of the cake. Leave to dry. Place the cake on the board.

2 Prepare the penguins: for each one, shape a small ball of black paste for the head and equal-sized pieces of white and black paste for the body. Colour a little white paste orange for the feet.

3 Lightly moisten one side of each of the two body pieces with glue and squash them together. Wipe off excess glue to avoid making a mess. Shape the body into a fat pear shape. Flatten the top and bottom. With tiny scissors, snip wing shapes in to the black paste and gently pull them into shape. Attach the head with a little water. Leave to dry for as long as possible.

4 Roll out the orange sugar paste and cut tiny circles for feet. Flatten one side and cut in half to make two webbed feet. Attach the feet with a little glue. Pipe white eyes and paint on black pupils. Make or pipe an orange beak. Attach the beak if necessary. Leave to set. Finally, dust yellow powder onto the breast – take care as it is very bright!

5 On the top of the cake, mark out an oval shape to make a run-out pond (page 37). Pipe the outline with slightly softened blue icing. When set, soften the royal icing to a flooding consistency and flood in the pond. Leave to set.

6 Gently add and rough up a little icing all around the top edge of the cake, allowing some to drip down the sides. Sprinkle with clear snowflake sparkles. Spread rough icing around the base of the cake on the board and add sparkles. Use a little white royal icing in a tiny bag to pipe fine lines of snow around the edges of the pond.

7 Attach the penguins on top and around the cake with royal icing. Trim the board with a ribbon.

Christmas by Starlight

This stunning design is simple and quick to make. The cut-outs and stars need a day or more to dry out, so do this before you cover the cake with marzipan and sugar paste. Add candles to the table for a really star-lit effect.

Serves 10-12

175g (6oz) bought flower paste mix

medium and small star cutters

gold cake wires

edible gold paint

snowflake and shooting star cutter or ruler

560g (1¼lb) Sugar Paste (page 30)

25cm (10in) round board

pale green edible food colouring

green sparkles

5cm (2in) Christmas tree cutter

Apricot Glaze (page 26)

450g (1lb) Marzipan (page 26)

20cm (8in) round Dark Rich Fruit Cake
    (page 20)

sparkly green ribbon

1 cellpick (cake insert to hold stems
    or wires)

1 Make up the flower paste according to the instructions on the packet. Roll out a little of the paste very thinly and cut out 30-40 stars of different sizes. Glue these on to gold wires, three to a wire and leave to set. Paint some of the stars gold.

2 Roll out a strip of flower paste. Emboss it with a snowflake or shooting star design and then use a small paintbrush to remove carefully. Attach some of these with glue to wires.

3 Use 110g (4oz) of the sugar paste for the trees: colour half with pale green colouring and green sparkles. Roll out to 3mm (⅛in) thick and cut out several Christmas trees in white and green. Leave to harden.

4 Brush the cake with apricot glaze. Cover with marzipan and then with sugar paste. Cover the board with sugar paste. While soft, emboss the cake sides and top with stars and snowflake patterns. Emboss the board. Paint some of the shooting stars, or the larger designs, with gold paint. Place the cake and board on a colourful base board or platter.

5 Tie a sparkly green ribbon around the cake. Attach the green trees over the ribbon, attaching them with glue or royal icing. Stand 3-4 white trees on the top of the cake and support them with icing.

6 Make a small hole in the top of the cake behind the trees and insert the cellpick in this. Arrange the wires with flying stars attached in the cellpick, taking care to ensure that the stars don't all fall off. If necessary, place a small piece of paste in the cellpick to keep the wires in place.

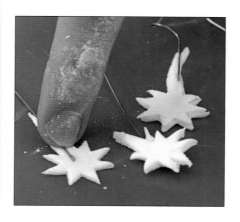

Yule Log

This is an excellent last-minute cake for Christmas. The Swiss roll can be made with any of the suggested flavours – chocolate is traditional but often just a bit too rich for some – a wholemeal sponge with nuts added makes a change. Make the sponge well in advance if you like, fill it with butter icing and freeze. Allow an hour for the cake to defrost before decorating.

Serves 8

3-egg Swiss Roll (page 17) made with
    wholemeal flour
25g (1oz) flaked almonds (or chopped
    mixed nuts)
1 quantity Butter Icing (page 23)
110g-175g (4-6oz) good dark chocolate
1tbsp cocoa powder
a little sifted icing sugar
1-2tsp boiled water

1 Make and bake the Swiss roll, adding the flaked almonds with the flour. Roll up, cool and unroll, then fill with half the butter icing and re-roll.

2 Melt the chocolate until smooth. Spread out in two or more batches on trays, a marble board or a clean work surface and flatten it evenly with a spatula. If your kitchen is warm, spread the chocolate on trays that can be moved to a cooler place.

3 Allow the chocolate to cool until it loses its shine. Keep testing the edges to check for setting so it does not cool too much and set hard. When it has set too much you will have to melt it again.

4 Use a clean paint stripper or wide metal spatula to push through the chocolate, making thick curls or cigar-type rolls, or thinner curls if you prefer. Put the curls in a cool place until required.

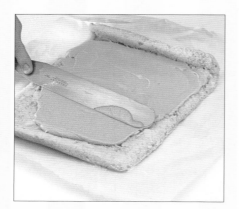

5 Blend the cocoa powder with the water and then beat this into the remaining butter icing. Beat well until really smooth, then spread thinly and evenly all over the Swiss roll.

6 Immediately arrange the chocolate curls neatly all over the cake to resemble a pile of logs. Dust with a little icing sugar if you wish and keep in a cool place until ready to serve.

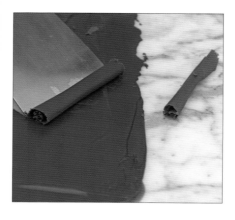

Happiness and Harmony Wedding Cake

Serves 20-30

23cm (9in) square Dark Rich Fruit Cake
   (page 20)
Apricot Glaze (page 26)
675g (1½lb) Marzipan (page 26)
675g (1½lb) Royal Icing (page 28)
cream edible food colouring (or mix tiny
   amounts of sunflower, chestnut and
   tangerine)
snowflake sparkle dust
bright pink carnations and greenery
gold and bright pink ribbons
28cm (11in) square board

The decoration on this cake is influenced by feng shui. The intertwined fishes represent harmony and peace, while fresh flowers add a splash of colour.

1 Brush the cake with apricot glaze and cover with marzipan. Coat with pale ivory cream coloured royal icing. Lightly ice the board. When all icing is dry, fix the cake in place on the board with royal icing.

2 Use the small template (page 96) to make four pairs of run-out fish in white royal icing and leave to set. When completely dry, dust with snowflake sparkle. Attach a gold ribbon and a thinner pink ribbon around the base of the cake.

3 Mark the top and sides in half, into triangles. With a no.1 nozzle, pipe fine snail piping along the base of the cake and up the sides at the corners. Outline the upper triangle with snail or zig-zag piping. Fill the triangle with cornelli piping (page 36).

4 Outline each triangle on the top of the cake with snail or zig-zag piping. Mark and pipe a large fish run-out directly onto the cake using the larger template (page 96). Fill in the second triangle with cornelli piping. Leave to dry.

5 Attach the small fish to the sides with royal icing. Leave to set thoroughly, then dust with a little more snowflake sparkle. Attach fresh flowers at the last moment.

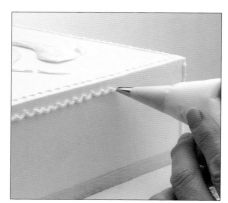

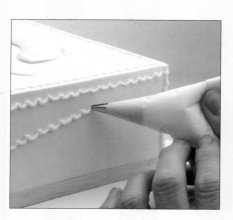

Love Birds Wedding Cake

Stunning birds in white and bronze make the perfect wedding cake top piece. Clever cutters are used to make the dove shapes and surprisingly simple piping with dramatic use of ribbons and bows completes the decoration.

Serves 100

15cm (6in), 20cm (8in) and 30cm (12in) round Dark Rich Fruit Cakes (page 20)
Apricot Glaze (page 26)
1kg (2¹/₂lb) Marzipan (page 26)
1kg (2¹/₂lb) Sugar Paste (page 30)
225g (8oz) pastillage or flower paste mix
225g (8oz) Royal Icing (page 28)
apricot or skin-tone edible food colour
copper and white satin lustre dust powders
dove patchwork cutters
Gildesol edible gilding medium
edible glue
floristry wire
white tape
bronze, apricot and white ribbons
35cm (14in) round cake board

Making Favours

To make favours, wrap apricot and bronzed sugared almonds in fine white netting and tie with very fine ribbon. To bronze the almonds, brush with Gildesol and bronze dust.

1 Brush all three cakes with apricot glaze and cover with marzipan. Cover them with varying shades of apricot sugar paste. Leave to firm up. Cover at least 5cm (2in) of the edge of the cake board with sugar paste and frill it with a fine cocktail stick or frilling tool.

2 Prepare the pastillage according to the packet instructions. Roll it out very thinly and cut out as many doves as possible – they are very fragile so it is a good idea to allow for breakages. Follow the instructions with the dove cutters to get good shape definition. Use a paintbrush to carefully remove the shapes from the cutters.

3 Cover wires with white tape and then carefully attach them to the backs of the doves with glue. Leave to set for several hours. Brush half the dove shapes with Gildesol and then brush with bronze satin dust. Brush the remaining dove shapes with Gildesol and white dust. Leave to set for several hours.

4 Cut a piece of fine graph paper long enough to go around the largest cake. Place this around the cake. Pin prick fine marks as a guide for the top and bottom of each line of dots. Mark the sides of the other cakes in the same way. Then pipe fine dots in rows around the sides of all three cakes. Leave to set.

5 Trim the edges of the cakes and the base board with bronze ribbon. Make two or three large ribbon bows and attach them to pieces of covered floristry wire.

6 Place the cakes on top of each other, set back, not centred. Very carefully place a bow on each side of the assembled cakes. Place two, four or more doves facing each other on the top cake. Add extra doves with the bows on either side of the lower tiers if you wish.

Templates

Piped Chocolate Decoration
(page 43)
Fairy Cakes (page 48)

Petal Power Cake (page 68)
Enlarge to 200% size for
20cm (8in) cake

Butterfly Thank You Cake
(page 70)

Simple Decoration for
Sponge Cake (page 18)
Enlarge to 200% size for
20cm (8in) cake

Happiness and Harmony
Wedding Cake
(page 92)